The Power of Bhagavad-gita

Stephen Knapp

Dedicated to
All seekers looking for the deepest spiritual truth,
and to my own spiritual master who gave such truth to me,
Srila A. C. Bhaktivedanta Swami Prabhupada.

Copyright © 2019, by Stephen Knapp

All rights reserved. No part of this book may be reproduced without written permission from the copyright owner and publisher, except for brief quotations for review or educational purposes.

All verses that are included are taken from the Bhagavad-gita As It Is by Srila A. C. Bhaktivedanta Swami Prabhupada, Bhaktivedanta Book Trust--International. Copyright © 1972.

COVER PHOTO: A print showing Lord Krishna explaining the wisdom of the Bhagavad-gita to His friend Arjuna, while on a chariot in the midst of the battlefield in Kurukshetra.

ISBN-13: 9781075257223

Published by
The World Relief Network,
Detroit, Michigan

You can find out more about Stephen Knapp and his books, free ebooks, research, and numerous articles and photos, along with many other spiritual resources at:
www.Stephen-Knapp.com
http://stephenknapp.info
http://stephenknapp.wordpress.com

Other books by the author:
1. The Secret Teachings of the Vedas: The Eastern Answers to the Mysteries of Life
2. The Universal Path to Enlightenment
3. The Vedic Prophecies: A New Look into the Future
4. How the Universe was Created and Our Purpose In It
5. Toward World Peace: Seeing the Unity Between Us All
6. Facing Death: Welcoming the Afterlife
7. The Key to Real Happiness
8. Proof of Vedic Culture's Global Existence
9. The Heart of Hinduism: The Eastern Path to Freedom, Enlightenment and Illumination
10. The Power of the Dharma: An Introduction to Hinduism and Vedic Culture
11. Vedic Culture: The Difference it can Make in Your Life
12. Reincarnation & Karma: How They Really Affect Us
13. The Eleventh Commandment: The Next Step for Social Spiritual Development
14. Seeing Spiritual India: A Guide to Temples, Holy Sites, Festivals and Traditions
15. Crimes Against India: And the Need to Protect its Ancient Vedic Tradition
16. Destined for Infinity, a spiritual adventure in the Himalayas
17. Yoga and Meditation: Their Real Purpose and How to Get Started
18. Avatars, Gods and Goddesses of Vedic Culture: Understanding the Characteristics, Powers and Positions of the Hindu Divinities
19. The Soul: Understanding Our Real Identity
20. Prayers, Mantras and Gayatris: A Collection for Insights, Protection, Spiritual Growth, and Many Other Blessings
21. Krishna Deities and Their Miracles: How the Images of Lord Krishna Interact with Their Devotees.
22. Defending Vedic Dharma: Tackling the Issues to Make a Difference.
23. Advancements of Ancient India's Vedic Culture.
24. Spreading Vedic Traditions Through Temples.
25. The Bhakti-yoga Handbook: A Guide to Beginning the Essentials of Devotional Yoga
26. Lord Krishna and His Essential Teachings
27. Mysteries of the Ancient Vedic Empire.
28. Casteism in India
29. Ancient History of Vedic Culture
30. A Complete Review of Vedic Literature
31. Bhakti-Yoga: The Easy Path of Devotional Yoga
32. The Power of the Maha-Mantra

CONTENTS

CHAPTER ONE: 1
THE IMPORTANCE OF THE BHAGAVAD-GITA
IN THIS DAY AND AGE

CHAPTER TWO: 12
APPLYING THE BHAGAVAD-GITA TO DAILY LIFE
    Principles for Good Management * The Bhagavad-gita and Principles of Good Leadership * Work Ethics in the Bhagavad-gita * Dealing with Stress * How to Control the Mind * How to Attain Peace of Mind * Heightening Self-Confidence and Self-Esteem * Dealing with Sorrow and Death * Attaining Fearlessness * The Key to Proper Foods for Health and Consciousness * Bhagavad-gita as a Psychological Guide * Acquiring Proper Knowledge * Meditation According to Bhagavad-gita * The Supreme Yoga * Options for Those Who Cannot Follow the Spiritual Path * Bhagavad-gita as a Key to Spiritual Enlightenment * Bhagavad-gita and Establishing World Peace

CHAPTER THREE: 57
THIRTY-ONE DAYS TO LIBERATION ON THE
VEDIC PATH
    Day One: Beginning Your New Life * Day Two: Why Be Absorbed in God? * Day Three: Have Faith and Keep Walking in the Light * Day Four: Transcendental Knowledge, The Way to Peace and Clarity * Day Five: Why This Knowledge is Given to You * Day Six: Learning Spiritual Truth Gives Proper Understanding * Day Seven: Follow the Purpose of Life * Day Eight: Be Diligent on the Path * Day Nine: Keep Adding Higher Qualities to Your

Character * Day Ten: Accept a Proper Spiritual Master * Day Eleven: Adjusting Your Diet for Higher Awareness * Day Twelve: You Are Not Your Body * Day Thirteen: You Are Eternal * Day Fourteen: Becoming Free From Bodily Desires * Day Fifteen: Attaining Spiritual Consciousness * Day Sixteen: There is Life After Death * Day Seventeen: Getting the Higher Taste of Spiritual Life * Day Eighteen: God Rewards You According to Your Deeds * Day Nineteen: Offering Service to God Brings Freedom * Day Twenty: How to Serve God * Day Twenty-one: Devotional Service to God Brings Moksha–Liberation * Day Twenty-two: What if I Cannot do it Right? * Day Twenty-three: Even if You Make a Mistake, You Are Saved * Day Twenty-four: Understanding the Divine Nature of God * Day Twenty-five: Understanding the Power of the Lord * Day Twenty-six: Staying Close to God * Day Twenty-seven: Tolerating Those who Don't Care for God * Day Twenty-eight: Your Special Position as God's Devotee * Day Twenty-nine: Be Great by Being an Example for Others * Day Thirty: Being Delivered at the Time of Death * Day Thirty-one: Sharing this Message

CHAPTER FOUR: **BHAGAVAD-GITA'S ULTIMATE PURPOSE**	105
CONCLUSION: **YOUR NEXT STEP**	113
GLOSSARY	115
INDEX	123
ABOUT THE AUTHOR	125
BOOKS BY STEPHEN KNAPP	128

CHAPTER ONE

The Importance of Bhagavad-gita in This Day and Age

Most everyone at some point hears about the *Bhagavad-gita*, but do they know what it really contains, or how profound and deep is the knowledge that it provides?

Besides being the classic Eastern text that it is, and the summary of most Upanishadic information, it is the core of the deepest levels of spiritual knowledge. It is also like a handbook for life. Just as when you purchase an appliance of some kind, like a refrigerator, television or computer, you get a manual that teaches you how to use it. So in the same way, if God created this world and put us here, doesn't it seem that He should also tell us what is the purpose of this life and how to use it accordingly? The *Bhagavad-gita* is such an instruction manual for anyone. It provides the basic answers that most people have about life, and the universal spiritual truths that can be used by anyone, anywhere, and at any time in history. In this way, it is timeless.

The purpose of the *Bhagavad-gita* is for universal well-being. It may have been spoken to Arjuna to alleviate his delusion about things, but it is meant for everyone. That is why it is important to study, understand and to apply its principles that continue to be timeless and relevant to many situations in modern life. In this way, it is also nonsectarian. It can be applied by anyone from any background, culture or religion for the benefits it offers.

Even in India, every spiritual leader or acharya from the different lineages have all taken benefit from the *Bhagavad-gita* and many have written commentaries on it. Not only does it offer spiritual knowledge, but many scientists have also found scientific insights in it. Thus, it is for the common people as well as scholars. The *Bhagavad-gita* emphasizes harmonious growth and development for everyone at all levels of life.

So let me explain a little of its importance and why we should take it seriously. I will not go into all of the details of what the *Bhagavad-gita* teaches, but I will provide a quick overview and summary of each chapter to give you an idea of the information you can discover and the benefits if you read it.

Of course, we know it was spoken on the battlefield at Kurukshetra as the forces prepared for war, a war meant to uphold the Dharmic principles against those who were bereft of them and before things became more evil than they already were, so there was little time in which to speak the *Bhagavad-gita*. Therefore, it was a brief conversation between Arjuna and Lord Krishna.

So, once the scene is set in the first chapter, from the second chapter it begins to explain some of the highest spiritual realizations known to humanity. It begins to explain exactly who and what we really are as spiritual beings. Without this knowledge in a person's life, the Vedic literature says that humans are little better than polished animals.

The reason for this conclusion is that human life is especially meant for spiritual inquiry because in no other species of life here on earth does the living being have the faculty, such as the intelligence and the means to understand spiritual knowledge. Otherwise, this implies that there is little difference in the purpose of life between humans and animals who are mostly interested in merely eating, sleeping, mating, and defending what they think is theirs.

However, human life is not merely the means to acquire knowledge from the teachings and explanations of others, but it also offers the facility to realize it within oneself by practice. It is a matter of uplifting one's consciousness so that one can perceive the higher dimensions that exist all around us. This is more than merely accepting something on faith alone, but it is a matter of attaining direct perception of what the Vedic literature discusses.

So, from the second chapter of the *Bhagavad-gita*, we begin to learn our real identity as the soul within these bodies. The *Bhagavad-gita* explains the size and nature of the soul, and how it is completely transcendental or beyond the body. It is beyond time and the effects of the three-dimensional world. It is beyond the limitations of the body and mind.

This teaches us many things. It shows that regardless of our physical limitations, we can rise above them because, spiritually, we are already above them. We simply have to realize that. What does it mean to realize it? It means to directly perceive that truth, to see it as plain as day. And then live according to that realization. This teaches us that regardless of our situation, socially or physically or economically, we can rise to higher levels of existence, both in this world and in the next.

This teaches us that no matter what kind of pressures we may feel from our classmates at school, or what good or bad biases that may come from our fellow workers, or what kind of labels they put on us, or how much they may purposefully demean or criticize us, or even how great we think we are, we can be grounded, fixed in understanding who and what we really are as a spiritual being inside the limited material body. That is how we should see ourselves. And then we can be confident that regardless of what others may say, we know who we are and can go through life fixed in perceiving our real identity and our purpose in this life and what really is our higher potential. As an old saying points out, it is better to see yourself truly than to care how others see you.

When you are spiritually grounded, it is no longer necessary to always try to convince others of your self-worth, or of your social status, or of trying to make it into the right clique or group of people. We become convinced of who we are. We work in our own way to provide a contribution to society, to make something of ourselves that has meaning, beyond the typical superficialities and meaningless and worldly gossip that occupy the minds of most people today. We know that as long as we keep working in our own way, both intellectually and spiritually, attaining the skills that will enable us to do something significant, that our time will come when we can make a mark on this world in our own sphere of influence, which may continue to expand from there.

So, we may be popular in school or not, or recognized in our career or not, but by our spiritual knowledge, as provided in the *Bhagavad-gita*, and by the confidence it gives us, we work to always become better, more uplifted, more refined, and more realized than we are, always making ourselves into a better person. Then we can help ourselves and others in more effective ways. This is just some of what the second chapter of the *Bhagavad-gita* can provide if we look into it carefully and understand who we really are and what is our greater potential.

As we proceed through the *Bhagavad-gita*, in Chapter Three, Lord Krishna discusses Karma-yoga, the knowledge of how every action creates an opposite and equal reaction. Fifty years ago in this country of the USA, hardly anyone spoke of karma, unless they were students of yoga or Eastern philosophy. Now everyone talks of karma, it is a part of the vocabulary, whether they really understand it or not. But the point is, where do you think that came from? How do you think they started to know about karma, or yoga for that matter, except for the fact that the teachings of the East and yoga, which are centered around the *Bhagavad-gita*, continued to spread throughout the West.

Similarly, considering all the knowledge that the *Bhagavad-gita* has within it, do you think that you will learn such things in the colleges or university courses? Hardly. You have to go beyond that. You have to take separate or alternative studies, like in studying the *Bhagavad-gita* or other Vedic texts, or listening to those who know about it. Then you can also begin to learn the basic laws of the universe as outlined in the *Bhagavad-gita*, as in the laws of karma. Otherwise, how will you begin to understand that your present circumstances and tendencies may be carry-overs from a previous existence? Or even from many previous existences that we have experienced. You only begin to understand these things by studying the *Bhagavad-gita*, the teachings of which are also expanded in the *Upanishads*, and then even more elaborated in the *Puranas* and other Vedic texts and commentaries.

In Chapter Four, called Transcendental Knowledge, it is explained to Arjuna how this knowledge was given and descends down through the *parampara* or disciplic succession. Lord Krishna explains the purpose and the transcendental nature of His appearance in this world. Also how to perform one's actions so they are spiritual activities, which can then enable a person to reach the spiritual abode.

In Chapter Five, Karma-yoga, Action in Krishna Consciousness, it is explained how to perform one's activities in the right consciousness of bhakti-yoga, and the way to focus on the natural, self-sufficient happiness within.

In Chapter Six, Sankhya-yoga, we find the instructions on how to conquer the mind to attain the natural inner happiness–beyond the senses–and become established in self-realization, the perception of one's real identity. And then to see all else, all things around you with a steady mind, free from desires and possessiveness.

Then Lord Krishna gives instructions on how to practice yoga and meditation so that we can eventually perceive the spiritual dimension all around us, of which we are a part. Then we can enter and experience boundless transcendental joy and bliss, free from maya or illusion, and in touch with the Supreme Consciousness. Then such a person can see God everywhere and every being in God. Thus, he is never lost.

In Chapter Seven, Knowledge of the Absolute, we have the instructions on how to know God, and how to see that everything rests and depends on God, like pearls strung on a thread. Also, how to recognize the power of God in all the powerful aspects of nature. Thus, we become aware of God and His potencies in all things around us until we reach the abode of God.

Chapter Eight, Attaining the Supreme. This chapter gives more specific information about the ways of material nature, how to get free of it, and how our consciousness at the time of death, developed by our thoughts, words and deeds, determines our next life, our next destination. Therefore, if we are remembering God, Krishna, then we can attain Him. So, the instructions include how to think of Lord Krishna and attain Him through devotional yoga. Also, there are instructions in how to understand the higher and eternal nature, beyond all matter, which is the ultimate destination of us all.

In Chapter Nine, The Most Confidential Knowledge, Lord Krishna gives advice that this spiritual knowledge is the king of all knowledge, the most secret of all secrets, and by following it we can attain direct perception of the self by realization. Lord Krishna goes on to explain how everything is working under Him, but fools will never be able to recognize this. But by engaging in devotional yoga, the mind becomes spiritualized enough to understand God as He is by realization, far beyond any mental speculation. Lord Krishna goes on to explain that He is impartial to all, but becomes a friend to those who offer loving service. By engaging in this process systematically, you can reach the highest abode.

In Chapter Ten, The Opulence of the Absolute, we find explanations on how everything, all spiritual and material worlds, emanate from the Absolute Truth–God. Those who know this engage in devotional yoga to God, and with that love, Lord Krishna gives them the understanding by which they can come to Him.

Then Lord Krishna tells Arjuna how He is situated in all the powers and powerful things throughout the universe, whether it is the radiant sun, the tranquil moon, the water of the ocean, the transcendental Om, the chanting of the holy names as in japa meditation, and in the immovable Himalayas, and much more. But it is only with a single fragment of His energy does Lord Krishna pervade and support this entire universe. This leads to...

Chapter Eleven, The Universal Form. It is in this chapter wherein Lord Krishna shows Arjuna, by giving Arjuna divine eyes, how He is spread throughout the entire universe by His energies and expansions. Some of what Arjuna sees is beautiful beyond compare, and other things that he sees in this universal form are terrible and frightening. Some are hundreds of thousands of multicolored divine forms, as well as demigods, planets, past and future events, and a splendor so bright it would equal hundreds of thousands of suns. Both birth and death could be seen within this amazing universal form that spread in all directions, both near and far throughout the universe.

This made Arjuna humble, who then requested Krishna to relieve him of this view and show him His four-armed form, and then again His more familiar and lovable two-armed form.

Now Arjuna was convinced that Lord Krishna was

the Supreme and everything both within and beyond this material manifestation, as well as the father and creator of this material manifestation.

Then in Chapter Twelve, Devotional Service, Lord Krishna explains the ultimate goal of life, and the essence of how to practice bhakti-yoga, focusing especially on how to serve and fix our mind and intelligence on the Supreme as Lord Krishna in all our activities and undertakings.

Then we have Chapter Thirteen, Nature, The Enjoyer, and Consciousness. This explains how the body is the center of the field of material activities, and how we should understand the body as the vehicle in which both the soul and Supersoul–Paramatma–reside. Also, that the body is not our real identity, but we should see through the body to recognize the living being within. The soul is beyond the body and illuminates the body by consciousness. This is the symptom of the soul within. Now we merely have to spiritualize our consciousness to directly perceive the soul, and then see the difference between the body and soul.

The field of activities also includes the five elements, ego, intelligence, the senses, mind, and various emotions that project from the mind, along with all moving and non-moving things. Aside from all this, Lord Krishna explains the characteristics of His expansion as the Supersoul and how to perceive Him within.

In Chapter Fourteen, The Three Modes of Material Nature, Lord Krishna describes the three modes or *gunas* and their characteristics as goodness (*sattva*), passion (*rajas*) and ignorance (*tamas*), and the nature of those persons according to how they are situated in each of these modes of nature. This also determines if one is progressing upward while acting in the mode of goodness, or simply maintaining while in the mode of passion, or regressing downward in ignorance or darkness. This analysis will also reveal the condition of one's next birth. As explained in verses 14 and 15 in this chapter: "When one dies in the mode of goodness, he attains the pure higher planets. When one dies in the mode of passion, he takes birth among those engaged in fruitive activities; and when he dies in the mode of ignorance, he takes birth in the animal kingdom."

So, the goal is to know how to act in order to rise above these three modes, which Lord Krishna clearly explains as being the process of devotional yoga.

Chapter Fifteen, The Yoga of the Supreme Person. Here Lord Krishna emphasizes how to engage in that yoga process which can elevate you to rise above all material inebriates and limitations, and material happiness and distress, in order to reach the spiritual abode.

Even though the living beings are all parts of the Lord, they are struggling very hard with the mind and the mental interpretations of our experiences within this material field of activities and the way we see ourselves in this world. Furthermore, until these conceptions are purified, they are carried from one body to the next, one life to the next, just as air carries aromas. One who is spiritually ignorant cannot understand how this takes place. But the progressing transcendentalist can clearly see all of this. Krishna also explains that one who knows Him as the Supreme Being knows everything and engages in devotional yoga to Him, and his endeavors will know perfection.

Chapter Sixteen, The Divine and Demoniac Natures. Here Lord Krishna makes it clear how to recognize the Divine qualities and actions, as well as the demoniac, both of which are in ourselves and in those around us. It is only the divine qualities that are conducive to spiritual progress and liberation, whereas the demoniac actions and qualities will keep you bound in material existence for many lifetimes. So, the next step is to associate with those of a divine nature and develop such qualities in ourselves, and avoid the demoniac. The demoniac can never approach God nor the spiritual world, but reach progressively lower forms of existence.

Chapter Seventeen, The Divisions of Faith. In this

chapter Lord Krishna explains that there are different kinds of faith and religions depending on what level of the modes of material nature are displayed by the living being, such as goodness, passion or ignorance. Therefore, some religions will be more materialistic, based on ego, or the bodily identification and attachment and pride, while others will be more spiritual. So, there is a difference between various religions, as explained in this chapter. They are not all the same, which sometimes people like to say. Lord Krishna describes the difference herein in a way we can clearly see the varieties and categories to which they belong. It is up to us to study this carefully to understand this.

So, as we go along in our study of these chapters, we begin to see a pattern or repetition in these teachings. There is much knowledge on various aspects of life and spiritual understanding, but time and again Lord Krishna expresses that it is He who is the Supreme Being, the creator of the universe, and it is He who should be the center of our worship and meditation. Furthermore, all of this knowledge is meant to raise our consciousness so we can return to the spiritual world. That is what this is for. Lord Krishna repeats this in several chapters herein. This is not some kind of philosophy to contemplate, but it is an action plan for the benefit of humanity so we can directly attain a spiritual vision and perceive the spiritual reality all around us, up to the point in which we can enter that spiritual domain, which is our real home. The material world is temporary and can never give the joy we are seeking. This is why Lord Krishna is explaining all of this, to motivate us to act according to His directions and attain the realm of eternal happiness and bliss, which is our eternal and constitutional nature. And He summarizes this in the final chapter of *Bhagavad-gita*.

Chapter Eighteen, The Conclusion, The Perfection of Renunciation, or Yoga of Renunciation for Moksha–Liberation from Material Existence. Herein Lord Krishna explains the way to become spiritually perfect through the proper means of renunciation or detachment from materialistic activities, but also how to continue with prescribed duties. Yet, out of all we may do or practice, Lord Krishna finally concludes with the instructions on the ultimate way of perfecting one's spiritual life and realize the highest truth, which is by performing devotional service, bhakti-yoga, and in this way rekindle one's loving relationship with God and then reach the eternal and imperishable spiritual abode.

In this way, a person can cross over all obstacles of conditional life by Lord Krishna's grace. Otherwise, a person will remain lost in the whirlpool of material existence. By surrendering unto Him, and then by His grace you can attain peace and the supreme abode. Lord Krishna then concludes that this is the most confidential of all knowledge given for your benefit. He instructs that if you think of Him, become His devotee, worship Him, just surrender unto Him, then you will be free from all sinful reactions and come to Him without fail.

It is further concluded that anyone who studies this conversation between Lord Krishna and Arjuna worships Lord Krishna with his or her intelligence. And simply by listening with faith to this conversation a person becomes free from sinful reaction and at least attains the planets of the pious.

So, these are the basic instructions that are related in the *Bhagavad-gita*, and some of the benefits of studying it. In this way, a person can acquire proper direction in life, a deeper realization of one's true identity, and attain a level of self-confidence and peace by inward reflection and realization that can never be reached through ordinary, materialistic studies or endeavors. Furthermore, these can be applied to assist us in all aspects of life to help bring us to our higher potential in everything we do, materially or spiritually. This is the power and the importance of the *Bhagavad-gita* and the instructions of Lord Krishna found within it.

CHAPTER TWO

Applying the Bhagavad-gita to Daily Life

So, if the *Bhagavad-gita* is so universal, how can we apply it to our daily lives? It is not a book filled only with lofty philosophy that may be so erudite that it can be hard to understand. The fact is that when this information is presented in the right context and in a simple way, we can see how it can be used in broadening our view of its applications and the way it can be incorporated into all aspects of life. Here are a few short examples of what advice we can find in it that can help us with our daily life.

PRINCIPLES FOR GOOD MANAGEMENT

The *Bhagavad-gita* also offers advice we can use in our common affairs, such as good principles for management. One thing it says is to work without personal attachment to the results, otherwise, when doing things out of the desire for mere personal gratification, such activities can become an impediment to reaching success. In other words, you should work for the greater good, or for a higher cause. As it explains, "While contemplating the objects of the senses, a person develops attachment for them, and from such attachment lust develops, and from lust anger arises. From anger, delusion arises, and from delusion bewilderment of memory. When memory is bewildered, intelligence is lost, and when intelligence is lost, one falls down again into the material pool." (Bg.2.62-63)

In other words, it is a pattern whereby when a person becomes overwhelmed with desire for achievement and does not immediately attain one's expectations, anger results. The person loses mental equilibrium which then proceeds to poor judgement and bad decisions. Then he or she loses sight of the real purpose of what he or she is doing, and also loses the ability to be a good leader. Then he or she falls down into the whirlpool of confusion and blindness to his or her own faults. Then sheer determination may drive you forward, but in the wrong direction.

So, if we crave power, money, position, adoration, excessive rewards, etc., we are already being misled by our own mentality. And we often become blind to the errors that we make. Therefore, we must remain focused on the higher goal and purpose, and develop non-attachment for personal credits and recognition or fruits of the activities. If money, power, responsibility, fame, comforts, etc., come automatically, then well and good. But that should not be our main purpose. We should perform our tasks and assignments for the sake of duty and not for outward fulfillment and selfish satisfaction. This does not mean that we are not motivated, but our purpose should be for the good of the company, the employees, or everyone involved, which means that everyone rises as success is reached. As explained further, "You have a right to perform your prescribed duty, but do not be attached to the fruits of action. Never consider yourself to be the cause of the results of your activities, and never be attached to inactivity or not doing your duty. Be steadfast in yoga [or your purpose], O Arjuna. Perform your duty and abandon all attachment to success or failure. Such evenness of mind is called yoga." (Bg.2.47-48) This is what paves the way for mental peace and the relief from stress, and toward good management. The goal should be for the upliftment of the whole team, for the accomplishment of the highest good.

Another point is that if we always work for the profit motive, then we get trapped by insatiable desires to acquire more and more. This can lead to taking up risky enterprises that will increase our stress and anxiety, which gradually is revealed to others no matter how equipoised we try to remain on the surface. This leads to poor management. This can also lead to selfishness to acquire the rewards even if it is at the expense of others. This never produces what is right or good. Plus, it always backfires on you sooner or later.

In this way, good management means that we lead our team to experience harmony, unity and cohesiveness. This leads to success rather than leading it into tension, turmoil, conflicts, discouragement, or low productivity, which leads to financial loss and high turnover. Everyone should share a similar vision and direction, and unity in planning and execution, and motivation and goal achievement, which leads to profit-making or profit-sharing. That also leads to long-term viability. According to the *Bhagavad-gita*, this is the basis of yoga and a spiritual state of mind from which everyone benefits.

THE BHAGAVAD-GITA AND PRINCIPLES OF GOOD LEADERSHIP

A leader in a company, or in politics, or of a team or institution must act as a role model for the rest of the members to follow. The *Bhagavad-gita* explains, "Whatever action is performed by a great man, common men follow in his footsteps. And whatever standards he sets by exemplary acts, all the world pursues." (Bg.3.21)

This is the importance of a leader, who must also practice the principles he expects of others and not be hypocritical. He should not simply expect others to do what he says, but not what he does. But he must show by example. He must be trustworthy and inspire others to be the same way and bring them to a higher standard of ethics and performance. Therefore, a true leader must be moral, righteous, virtuous, positive, and dynamic. Then he will not be blamed for unrighteous behavior.

Some of the qualities that are outlined in the *Bhagavad-gita* for a true leader, as explained by Lord Krishna, are, "Humility, pridelessness, nonviolence, tolerance, simplicity, approaching a genuine spiritual master [for proper knowledge], cleanliness, steadiness and self-control; renunciation of [or freedom from] the objects of sense gratification, absence of false ego, the perception of the evil of [or the trouble in the process of the continued rounds of] birth, old age, disease and death; non-attachment to children, wife, home and the rest, and even-mindedness amid pleasant and unpleasant events, constant and staunch devotion to Me [God], resorting to solitary places [for peace of mind], detachment from the general mass of people; accepting the importance of spiritual self-realization, and the philosophical search for the Absolute Truth [as the goal of life]–all these I thus declare to be knowledge, and what is contrary to these is ignorance." (Bg.13.8-12)

Having these qualities will help a leader to be dynamic, virtuous, truthful, a visionary, and strong enough to keep the dream or goal in focus and make it into a reality, and be capable of recognizing the talents of others and bringing good people to reaching success with their own abilities.

Arjuna, in *Bhagavad-gita*, although he was more capable than anyone in today's world, had still reached a stage of confusion about what he should do. He was about to abandon his duties, give up the fight, and simply run from the battlefield to retire in the forest. But that was not what Lord Krishna wanted him to do. In fact, Krishna told Arjuna he was simply acting like a fool, and then Krishna took the time to explain the whole *Bhagavad-gita* to him to relieve his anxiety, his delusion, and bring him to the stage of spiritual realization and understanding of what was his real purpose. Thus, the *Bhagavad-gita* can do the same for us.

Krishna's message uplifted Arjuna's mind to abandon his inertia, stimulate his thinking, and inspire him to take up his duty and follow the righteous path. This is an example of a real leader. Finally, Lord Krishna tells Arjuna that he can make his own decision to act according to Krishna's instruction or not. But Arjuna then says, "My dear Krishna, O infallible one, my illusion is now gone. I have regained my memory by Your mercy, and I am now firm and free from doubt and am prepared to act according to Your instructions." (Bg.18.73) This is the potency of the spiritual message of *Bhagavad-gita*.

WORK ETHICS IN BHAGAVAD-GITA

The *Bhagavad-gita* also has some verses that shed some light on the proper work ethics we should have. For one thing, we should not be lazy, but should be ready to work, for while we are in this material world without work we can hardly maintain our own body. "Perform your prescribed duty, for action is better than inaction. A man cannot even maintain his physical body without work." (Bg.3.8)

How we should perform our occupation and the qualities we should have while doing so is also outlined: "Nonviolence, truthfulness, freedom from anger; renunciation, tranquility, aversion to faultfinding, compassion and freedom from covetousness, gentleness, modesty and steady determination; vigor, forgiveness, fortitude, cleanliness, freedom from envy and the passion for honor–these transcendental qualities, O son of Bharata, belong to godly men endowed with divine nature." (Bg.16.2-3) These are qualities we should all try to acquire.

The qualities we should avoid and the type of persons who have these qualities are also given: "Arrogance, pride, anger, conceit, harshness and ignorance–these qualities belong to those of demonic nature." (Bg.16.4)

So, this advice is very clear and is easy to apply. We only need to adjust our consciousness and try to attain the above-mentioned good characteristics and implement them in our daily life, and things will go much more smoothly for ourselves, and in our interactions with others.

DEALING WITH STRESS

The *Bhagavad-gita* has some practical information about dealing with something so common as stress. This is something we all may feel at various points in our life, and there have been many doctors, psychologists, and writers who have offered their theories and remedies on how we can reduce our stress.

We may encounter stress in the workplace, or at school, in driving on the highway, or with meeting deadlines with projects, or in simply dealing with others, and in so many other aspects of life. In some ways, stress may not be so bad if it is a motivator to get ourselves inspired to get something accomplished or to meet challenges, or to be more than we are at present.

However, too much stress can cause health problems like high blood pressure, headaches, or cause things like worry, depression, anxiety, all of which can deplete our energy or even shorten our duration of life. So, it has to be controlled to some degree and not be a major contender for our state of being or mental balance.

To decrease our stress, the *Bhagavad-gita* focuses on changing our view of things like who we are and our place in the world. It also recommends a good diet, as described later. But how do we change our attitude in a way that can help reduce our stress?

One of the things that is mentioned in the *Bhagavad-gita* is: "One who is not disturbed in spite of the threefold miseries, who is not elated when there is happiness, and who is free from attachment, fear and anger, is called a sage of steady mind." (Bg.2.56)

This points out a few things, beginning with not being disturbed by the threefold miseries. These include, 1.) the miseries caused by the body. Just having a body alone will cause so many problems, whether it be in maintaining it, keeping it healthy, or dealing with the pains that are common to having a physical body, such as headaches, toothaches, stomach problems, and so on. Then there is, 2.) the problems caused by others who we encounter. It is natural that there will be problems caused by other beings, such as barking dogs, biting insects, large animals that may attack us, noisy neighbors, or other people who do not get along with us, or in things like paying rent to the landlord or taxes to the government. So many issues can take place in our dealing with others that can make life unpleasant. Then 3.) is the problems that come from nature. These may include blistery winters, heavy storms, hurricanes, tornadoes, floods, forest fires, droughts, and so much more.

The thing is we have to expect these. They are automatic. These are part of life. All we can do is try to reduce their effects as much as possible, but we cannot completely stop them for these will affect us no matter where in the world we are. But when we know what they are, we can also watch them come and go into and out of our lives. As the *Bhagavad-gita* also explains, happiness and sadness come and go like the winter and summer seasons. "The nonpermanent appearance of happiness and distress, and their disappearance in due course, are like the appearance and disappearance of winter and summer seasons. They arise from sense perception, O scion of Bharata, and one must learn to tolerate them without being disturbed." (Bg.2.14)

Herein it explains that one season may be more pleasant than another, as interpreted by our mind and senses, but they both will come and go as a normal course of events. Neither of them are permanent. We can only tolerate them and not let them affect us too much. We should not let ourselves become overly elated when there is happiness, or too sorrowful when there are reversals in life. This will help us remain free from fear and anger, and keep our mind steady in all situations. But that takes understanding and control of our own perspective of things. As the *Bhagavad-gita* further says: "He who is without attachment, who does not rejoice when he obtains good, nor lament when he obtains evil, is firmly fixed in perfect knowledge." (Bg. 2.57)

"One who is able to withdraw his senses from sense objects, as the tortoise draws his limbs within the shell, is to be understood as truly situated in knowledge." (Bg.2.58)

This is part of the goal of living a stress-free lifestyle. In other words, when we are focused on identifying with our spiritual identity within, we can withdraw our senses from being focused only on the drama that may be going on around us, like the tortoise in the shell as the example the *Bhagavad-gita* uses. Then we remain steady in our disposition and spiritual identity, and in this way be situated in knowledge. But what is this knowledge?

It is acting in this world but knowing we are not of it. We are more than this, higher than our set of circumstances, which are ever-changing. You may endeavour to accomplish something, but success or failure does not determine who you are or your external identity, unless you believe it to be.

For example, you may be a successful sports player, having earned many rewards. And you may believe this is your real identity, and why people appreciate and value you, which matters very much to you. But then you may suffer an injury or simply grow old with age, which now prevents you from performing as well as you used to. Does that mean your identity has changed? Are you no longer worth as much as you used to be? Do you view yourself differently? Why? Because you have put so much into the external identity of yourself, which is always changing from the moment you are born until the time that you die. It is automatic, like the threefold miseries that were previously described. It is a part of life, and you have to flow with it. And you have to be flexible enough to go with the flow.

However, understanding your inner or spiritual identity, which always stays the same, gives you the perspective that you are acting and watching the results that take place, but you are not the results or the changes themselves. You can simply observe and be flexible enough to roll with the changes that go on around you. Then they are not so serious, but only if you remain somewhat detached, like a tourist traveling through a new or strange land. You then think, "So, this is how things go on here. This is what this place is like," knowing full well you will be someplace else later. You do not become attached to what is happening around you. That does not mean you do not try to make things better for others, or put forth positive changes, but it means you can tolerate the fluctuations that are a constant factor, which will greatly help give you freedom from stress.

So, the natural means of reducing stress, without resorting to drugs, prescriptions, therapy, etc., is to simply change our perspective of who we are and what is our place in the world, and how we interact with our surroundings. This is being situated in spiritual understanding. But this is also connected with controlling the mind, which we may have to do until we are more fully situated in spiritual knowledge, which we will discuss next.

HOW TO CONTROL THE MIND

One of the most widespread problems is simply the way the mind can take us to all kinds of ideas, doubts, pessimism, worries, or hopes, dreams, etc., some of which may be reasonable, but others not so much. And this may also take away what happiness we could otherwise have if not for the wild journeys of the mind, such as being preoccupied with the past, or worried about the future, and not being able to stay in the moment. Sometimes we cannot even absorb what we read or hear because our mind becomes so strong that we can't stop the internal conversation that goes on which demands our attention. Then somebody may be talking to us, but we are thinking about how to respond so much that we fail to hear what is said.

So, how can we begin to get free of the constant ramblings of the mind? Even Arjuna said in the *Bhagavadgita* (6.34) it is easier to try and control the wind. "For the mind is restless, turbulent, obstinate and very strong, O Krishna, and to subdue it is, it seems to me, more difficult than controlling the wind."

Nonetheless, in this regard, "The Blessed Lord said: O mighty-armed son of Kunti, it is undoubtedly very difficult to curb the restless mind, but it is possible by constant practice by detachment." (Bg.6.35)

Herein it is by constant practice that the mind can be subdued, and also by reducing the material desires that the mind dictates to us as goals we need to satisfy. These actually occupy the mind with so many unnecessary thoughts. Becoming free of them will naturally help subdue the mind. However, by what kind of practice can we curb the mind's wandering? It is further explained, "From whatever and wherever the mind wanders due to its flickering and unsteady nature, one must certainly withdraw it and bring it back under the control of the Self." (Bg.6.26)

The Self means the higher intellect. By cultivated knowledge acquired from study or hearing, we learn what we should or should not do, or what we should not think about. Therefore, the mind can be like a television, meaning that if you are watching something you do not like, or that is distasteful or a waste of time, you simply change the channel. Similarly, by this verse in *Bhagavad-gita*, if we notice that our mind has wandered to a dark place or is contemplating negative thoughts, we simply bring our thoughts up to a higher level, or bring it back to think about something more positive. We change the channel.

In this way, we control the mind and can actually elevate ourselves to reach a higher consciousness, as explained, "A man must elevate himself by his own mind, not degrade himself. The mind is the friend of the conditioned soul, and his enemy as well. For him who has conquered the mind, the mind is the best of friends, but for one who has failed to do so, his very mind will be the greatest enemy." (Bg.6.5-6)

What is especially effective is when we bring our mind not only to more positive thoughts or subjects, but when we want to dwell on what is more spiritual. This is taught by Lord Krishna, "One who restrains his senses and fixes his consciousness upon Me is known as a man of steady intelligence." (Bg.2.61) Then the mind can become balanced, equipoised, steady, and elevated. It then becomes our friend. This can never happen when contemplating the constant drama of activities or ups and downs in the material realm.

So, no matter whether we are simply trying to acquire a steady mind for material or spiritual purposes, this is a most simple method of doing that. As further stated, "For one who is so situated in the Divine consciousness, the threefold miseries of material existence exist no longer; in such a happy state, one's intelligence soon becomes steady." (Bg.2.65) Now who would not want that? In this way, controlling the mind is also the means to become happy.

Therefore, this is a basic process in how we can begin to control our mind. And without controlling the mind, there can be no peace. And the lack of mental peace is reflected and projected outside ourselves in all of our other relations and activities. So, attaining peace of mind is what we will describe next.

HOW TO ATTAIN PEACE OF MIND

Without peace of mind, there can be no happiness. When a person is always agitated, he can never know peace, and without peace, what is the question of happiness? This is a basic premise in the *Bhagavad-gita*.

The fact is that it is impossible to attain any real peace of mind while absorbed in the constant changes of material nature and the ever-fluctuating activities that go on within it. Of course, some people may say that without these constant ups and downs, life would be boring. Some say it is the challenges that test you, that push you to become better, or to attain new talents and become a more developed person. So, it has its place. Even the feeling of accomplishment is a kind of peace, or relief, or a sense of victory, that you have finally made it. But that is different than simply being at peace with yourself and the world.

On the other hand, many of the changes that take place in our lives are things that we do not desire. But sometimes you cannot help it, you have to deal with situations as they come up, which may be anything but peaceful. And as long as we are completely focused or involved in the affairs or activities that go on in materialistic society, or the world in general, there is no chance of ever really experiencing a truly peaceful state of mind. There is always something that will keep you agitated or concerned about what is going to happen, either in the field of the world's economy, or in politics, international affairs, social development or the lack of it, or stormy changes in the weather, or how your debts can be paid, and on and on. As it says, "One who is not in transcendental consciousness can have neither a controlled mind nor steady intelligence, without which there is no possibility of peace. And how can there be any happiness without peace?" (Bg.2.66)

So, how do we tolerate this and stay mentally equipoised? The first part of the solution is advised herein that we begin to lighten our load of materialistic concerns to help us become unagitated: "A person who is not disturbed by the incessant flow of desires–that enter like rivers into the ocean which is ever being filled but is always still–can alone achieve peace, and not the man who is always striving to satisfy such desires." (Bg.2.70)

This does not mean that we give up or run away from the responsibilities that we have accepted. You cannot use spirituality as an excuse to give up your obligations, such as being a father or mother when you already have children, etc. But you can begin to change your perspective and live life as a means to accomplish only those things that are most important, and those for which you have time. Everything else can fall by the wayside.

We obviously do not have time to do everything. So, we have to choose those things which are the most essential. And as our field of activities narrow, our concerns also become fewer, and peace of mind becomes easier to attain. As stated in the *Bhagavad-gita*, "Therefore, O mighty-armed, one whose senses are restrained from their objects [of desire] is certainly of steady intelligence." (Bg.2.68)

The idea in the *Bhagavad-gita* is that we begin to change our taste for happiness from the material or sensual pleasures to the higher spiritual joys. Then our consciousness also becomes more refined. "The embodied soul may be restricted from sense enjoyment, though the taste for sense objects remains. But, ceasing such engagements by experiencing a higher taste, he is fixed in consciousness." (Bg.2.59) The point is to attain a higher level of joy and happiness by developing our spiritual awareness. Material happiness may provide some excitement, but it is always temporary with a beginning and end, while the spiritual taste within is always increasing. We only have to tune into it.

So, as we continue to develop in this way, the external ups and downs of life will be perceived by us as becoming less drastic. As it is further explained: "He who is without attachment, who does not rejoice when he obtains good, nor lament when he obtains evil, is firmly fixed in perfect knowledge." (Bg.2.57) In other words, the person becomes fixed and steady in his or her view of the surrounding changes.

In this way, all things become more tolerable and we begin to feel contentment. A person who is content is at peace, and such a content person can find happiness wherever he goes. Another verse that shows this line of thinking is, "A person who has given up all desires for sense gratification [or external activities], who lives free from desires [in contentment], who has given up all sense of proprietorship and is devoid of false ego–he alone can attain real peace." (Bg.2.71)

Of course, as we continue to age, many of our concerns automatically fall away, like when our children grow up and move away, or when the need to maintain a big house is no longer necessary, we can begin to become free from such responsibilities. Then we become freer to pursue an easier life of contentment and for developing our spiritual awareness. "A faithful man who is absorbed in transcendental knowledge and who subdues his senses quickly attains the supreme spiritual peace." (Bg.4.39)

However, we do not necessarily need to wait for attaining old age. How much peace we can attain all depends on how much and how fast we want to develop in this way. We can become free from the burden of materialistic concerns even while at the heights of our career, for example, merely by learning how to separate our external or sensual realm of consciousness from our inner or spiritual realm. Meditation or contemplating the teachings of the *Bhagavad-gita* are a few of the ways we can do this. By this process, we may act in this world but fully know what is our spiritual identity as the soul within, and in this way withdraw into ourselves and our peace of mind at any time while still upholding our material duties and obligations. As the *Bhagavad-gita* explains, "Such a liberated person is not attracted to material sense pleasure or external objects but is always in trance [or in focus], enjoying the pleasure within. In this way, the self-realized person enjoys unlimited happiness, for he concentrates on the Supreme." (Bg.5.21)

This gives us some indications that by using this method of practice, peace of mind is attainable, or at least becomes more easily accessible for us.

HEIGHTENING SELF-CONFIDENCE AND SELF-ESTEEM

Unfortunately, there may be times in our life when we lose self-confidence or develop a low opinion of ourselves, or even become critical of things we have done. In some ways this can be good to re-evaluate our situation and purpose, our goals, who we are and where we want to go or what we wish to accomplish in life. That is also called *svadhyaya* in Sanskrit, or the study of ourselves and our position in this world, and to reach the understanding of being a spirit soul in a material body.

This can have a positive effect, but if we simply become despondent because of a feeling of uselessness, or that we have nothing to offer, or that no one appreciates us, then we are simply drifting into the illusion and are allowing wrong conceptions of ourselves to rule our mind and thinking. This can happen when we lose sight of what and who we really are. It does not matter so much about what other people think of us. What matters is understanding how we fit into reality. Remember, it is more important to see ourselves clearly than to care how others see us. This is what the *Bhagavad-gita* teaches.

To get to the point, you are here only because you have a purpose. You may not be so aware of what that purpose is right now, but it is true. Otherwise you would not be here. And part of our purpose for being here is to understand why we are here. In spite of everything else a person may accomplish, what is the point of being well-known, or so appreciated, wealthy, talented, all of which may be nice, yet to remain so shallow that he or she does not know who and what he is? Without that, it is considered that all of one's education is incomplete, and their human life is wasted.

You have to be centered in your true identity to be able to handle everything that goes on around you, or to have singleness of purpose in the direction you wish to take in this world. We have already explained a little about that. But now you need to know that you, as a spirit soul within a material body, are also a particle of the Supreme Spirit, the Absolute Truth, which is something far bigger and more important than you can imagine. It is far superior than all the other superficial things you could be or that you can accomplish.

To understand this is the true purpose of human existence. Other animals do not have the capacity or intelligence to understand and realize their spiritual identity, and then follow the process that allows them to enter into the spiritual realm. Most beings, and even most humans, are simply focused on the means to more efficiently eat, sleep, have sex and children, defend their lives from others who threaten them, and then grow old and die. For what? Where do you go from there? Yet, somehow you have attained a human birth, and this is your opportunity to reach spiritual realization of who and what you really are, far above and beyond simply eating, sleeping, mating, defending, and then dying.

So, you as a human being are far more important than you realize. You simply have to focus on what matters most now that you have attained this human existence. Then you can realize that we all are connected to and have a relationship with God. No one can take that away from you. Not any institution, church, or preacher can take that away because that is your eternal position. You only need to awaken that realization by acquiring the right knowledge, which is the purpose of the *Bhagavad-gita*, which is to help you do that. As Lord Krishna says. "And when you have thus learned the truth, you will know that all living beings are but part of Me–and that they are in Me, and are Mine." (4.35)

To give an illustration of what this means and how special we are as part of the Absolute Truth, we can use one of the most fantastic parts of *Bhagavad-gita*, in Chapter Eleven, where Krishna shows Arjuna His universal form, which spreads throughout the universe in amazing displays of energy. But know that we are a part of that energy, we are a part of the universal form. And herein Krishna also explains what is our purpose as part of this form.

"The Blessed Lord said: My dear Arjuna, O son of Pritha, behold now My opulences, hundreds of thousands of varied divine forms, multicolored like the sea. O best of the Bharatas, see here the different manifestations of Adityas, Rudras, and all the demigods. Behold the many things which no one has ever seen or heard before. Whatever you wish to see can be seen all at once in this body. This universal form can show you all that you now desire, as well as whatever you may desire in the future. Everything is here completely." (Bg.11.5-7)

"Arjuna saw in that universal form unlimited mouths and unlimited eyes. It was all wondrous. The form was decorated with divine, dazzling ornaments and arrayed in many garbs. He was garlanded gloriously, and there were many scents smeared over His body. All was magnificent, all-expanding, unlimited. This was seen by Arjuna. If hundreds of thousands of suns rose up at once into the sky, they might resemble the effulgence of the

Supreme Person in that universal form. At that time Arjuna could see in the universal form of the Lord the unlimited expansions of the universe situated in one place although divided into many, many thousands." (Bg.11.11-13)

"Arjuna said: My dear Lord Krishna, I see assembled together in Your body all the demigods and various other living entities [including all humans]. I see Brahma sitting on the lotus flower as well as Lord Shiva and many sages and divine serpents... There is no end, there is no beginning, and there is no middle to all this." (Bg.11.15-16)

"You are the supreme primal objective; You are the best in all the universes; You are inexhaustible, and You are the oldest; You are the maintainer of religion, the eternal Supreme Person. You are the origin without beginning, middle or end. You have numberless arms, and the sun and moon are among Your great unlimited eyes. By Your own radiance You are heating this entire universe... O Vishnu, I see You devouring all people in Your flaming mouths and covering the universe with Your immeasurable rays. Scorching the winds, You are manifest." (Bg.11.18-19, 30)

"The Blessed Lord said: Time I am, destroyer of the worlds, and I have come to engage all people." (Bg.11.31)

Herein Lord Krishna indicates that we are part of the plan of God, and also hints at the purpose of the cosmic creation, which is to engage all people in allowing them to pursue their material desires until they become tired and frustrated with such pursuits and then begin to ask the question "why am I here?" Any time we ask ourselves why is this happening to me, or why has this turned out like this, or why am I suffering, and so on, it is simply another form of asking the same question, "why am I here?" Then, after reaching such a stage in their development, if they are fortunate, Krishna arranges the means by which they can begin to understand their real position in life as a spiritual being enveloped in the material energy. If they can comprehend this, they can begin to perceive how they are far more than a temporary form, but are an eternal spiritual being, capable of entering the spiritual domain to leave this temporary world behind once and for all.

Arjuna continued: "You are the original Personality of Godhead. You are the only sanctuary of this manifested cosmic world. You know everything, and You are all that is knowable. You are the material modes. O limitless form! This whole cosmic manifestation is pervaded by You!" (Bg.11.38)

"You are air, fire, water, and you are the moon! You are the supreme controller and grandfather. Thus I offer my respectful obeisances unto You a thousand times, and again and again.!" (Bg.11.39)

In this way, we can understand how Krishna's energies are all pervasive, and we are a part of the Supreme, and will always be a part of the Supreme. Therefore, there is no reason to feel depressed, low, or as if we have no purpose in this world or reason for being here. We have always had a purpose, though we only need to be reawakened to what that purpose is and what to do to achieve it. And the message in the *Bhagavad-gita* is the means to understand what that purpose is.

So, if we are not feeling confident in ourselves or what we are doing, the instructions of the *Bhagavad-gita* will help pull us out of such doldrums and can inspire us to comprehend that we are much more than we may give ourselves credit for. And we are part of something much bigger than ourselves. Studying such a text as the conversation between Lord Krishna and Arjuna is the means to attain our original spiritual identity, beyond this body and this temporary world, and understand who or what is God and what is our connection with God, and then attain our real home in the spiritual realm. How can we do that is repeated by Lord Krishna in His instructions in *Bhagavad-gita* as we find here:

"My dear Arjuna, only by undivided devotional

service can I be understood as I am, standing before you [now in My two-armed form], and can thus be seen directly. Only in this way can you enter into the mysteries of My understanding. My dear Arjuna, one who is engaged in My pure devotional service, free from the contamination of previous activities [or karma] and from mental speculation, who is friendly to every living entity, certainly comes to Me." (Bg.11.54-55)

DEALING WITH SORROW AND DEATH

Death itself is never a pleasant topic, but we all have to face it, whether it be our own death, or the death of those around us. We cannot escape it, though many would like to. But we have to remember that death is but a portal to the next realm, to the next step toward our ultimate destination. As it is said, life is but a moment on our great path toward self-realization and ultimate liberation into the spiritual realm.

This means that though the body is temporary, the soul, our real identity is eternal. And this is clearly explained by Lord Krishna in the *Bhagavad-gita*. This is some of what He says in His explanations to Arjuna, which is good for all of us to consider:

"Those who are wise lament neither for the living nor the dead. Never was there a time when I did not exist, nor you, nor all these kings; nor in the future shall any of us cease to be. As the embodied soul continually passes in this body, from boyhood to youth to old age, the soul similarly passes into another body at death. The self-realized soul is not bewildered by such a change." (Bg.2.11-13)

In this way, for those of us who can understand this, we see that death is but a natural course of events, part of the cycle that allows us to move forward. When we have accomplished all we are meant to do in this life, there is no reason to continue to stay. It is time to move on to our next level of progress as we proceed to our final destination. The sage who can understand this is not confused nor saddened by such a change.

Krishna continues to explain: "Know that which pervades the entire body is indestructible. No one is able to destroy the imperishable soul. Only the material body of the indestructible, immeasurable and eternal living entity is subject to destruction... He who thinks that the living entity is the slayer or that he is slain, does not understand. One who is in knowledge knows that the self slays not nor is slain. For the soul there is never birth nor death. Nor, having once been, does he ever cease to be. He is unborn, eternal, ever-existing, undying and primeval. He is not slain when the body is slain." (Bg.2.17-20)

"As a person puts on new garments, giving up old ones, similarly, the soul accepts new material bodies, giving up the old and useless ones. The soul can never be cut into pieces by any weapon, nor can he be burned by fire, nor moistened by water, nor withered by the wind. This individual soul is unbreakable and insoluble, and can be neither burned nor dried. He is everlasting, all-pervading, unchangeable, immovable and eternally the same. It is said that the soul is invisible, inconceivable, immutable, and unchangeable. Knowing this, you should not grieve for the body." (Bg.2.22-25)

"O descendant of Bharata, he who dwells in the body is eternal and can never be slain. Therefore you need not grieve for any creature." (Bg.2.30)

Therefore, one of the greatest mysteries for us to realize is our own eternal nature as a spiritual being. The Vedic texts consider this is the ultimate goal of human existence. And this perception will certainly help relieve us of the fear or grief that may accompany death.

ATTAINING FEARLESSNESS

Now that we understand a little more about who and what we are, and what is the ultimate purpose and goal of human life, and how we are always connected with God, we can move forward fearlessly. When we actually realize this, and can see that the material creation is all part of God's energies, we can begin to feel that we are already home. We are not lost to God, nor is God lost to us. And nothing will change that. As stated, "For one who sees Me everywhere and sees everything in Me, I am never lost, nor is he ever lost to Me." (Bg.6.30)

Nonetheless, there may be many reasons why we become fearful at times. We are afraid of pain, suffering, loss, etc., but one of the main sources of fear is simply the fear of the unknown. The ultimate unknown is the future. And the ultimate future is what lies beyond death. That is why it is said that all fear is merely the reflection of the fear of death.

In overcoming the fear of death, developing spiritual knowledge and understanding, which also means to raise our consciousness, is one of the most effective means to overcome fear. We can then get an understanding of what lies beyond death. In fact, as Lord Krishna explains in *Bhagavad-gita* (2.40): "In this endeavor there is no loss or diminution, and a little advancement on this path can protect one from the most dangerous type of fear."

This means that any spiritual advancement is never lost at any stage. Unlike material endeavors that have to be completed and successful in this lifetime, spiritual progress belongs to the soul, and can thus be taken with us from one life to the next. We never lose it but keep adding to our progress. In this way, we can move forward in fearlessness knowing that sooner or later, whether in a few or in many lifetimes, we will ultimately reach the goal of attaining the spiritual realm, free from any further births in material existence. This is real fearlessness.

As Lord Krishna further explains: "Being freed from attachment, fear and anger, being fully absorbed in Me and taking refuge in Me, many, many persons in the past became purified by knowledge of Me–and thus they all attained transcendental love for Me." (Bg.4.10)

"And whoever, at the time of death, quits his body, remembering Me alone, at once attains My nature. Of this there is no doubt." (Bg.8.5)

Much more can be said about this, but in summary, this is the knowledge that can erase all fear of the future and of death. Thus, we can move forward with confidence.

THE KEY TO PROPER FOODS FOR HEALTH AND CONSCIOUSNESS

The *Bhagavad-gita* also gives advice on the proper kinds of food we should eat for developing our health and consciousness. It explains: "Foods in the mode of goodness increase the duration of life, purify one's existence and give strength, health, happiness and satisfaction. Such nourishing foods are sweet, juicy, fattening and palatable. Foods that are too bitter, too sour, salty, pungent, dry and hot, are liked by people in the modes of passion. Such foods cause pain, distress, and disease. Food cooked more than three hours before being eaten, which is tasteless, stale, putrid, decomposed and unclean, is food liked by people in the mode of ignorance." (Bg.17.8-10)

What many people do not realize is that food can affect our consciousness in different ways, which can also affect our moods. Furthermore, too many times we see people suffering disease and ill health while not even knowing that much of their condition is caused by their own eating habits and lifestyle. If they changed that, it could make a real difference. And here Lord Krishna is giving advice that the right foods of sweet fruits, wholesome grains and fresh vegetables, along with medicinal herbs and leaves, can increase our happiness, health, mental and intellectual sharpness, and our duration of a productive life.

When He says fattening foods, He does not simply mean cakes and ice cream and the like. No. But He means foods that are naturally healthy for the body and gives us stamina and endurance and strength. They give substance to the body and not simply fill it with empty calories.

Krishna also advises the foods to be avoided, that will have negative effects on us. Of course, only 30 years ago we did not have to worry about GMO foods and the pesticides that many foods carry today. To be healthy, we now also need to avoid these foods as well. Foods can be like medicine that give us the nutrition we need to lead a balanced and healthy life, which is good for spiritual development. Otherwise, a poor choice of foods, as briefly described in this verse, can be like poison.

BHAGAVAD-GITA AS A PSYCHOLOGY GUIDE

In Latin *psycho* means the soul and *logy* means study. So, psychology actually means the study of the soul and the ways it interacts through the mind and senses, or physical body. This is explained most effectively in Chapter 13 of the *Bhagavad-gita* on "Nature, the Enjoyer and Consciousness." This helps explain how the soul is situated in the body and interacts through it. Understanding this will automatically explain so many of the challenges we face in our situations.

Unfortunately, modern psychology questioned how the soul can neither be seen nor touched, so how can it be studied? Therefore, the study of the soul was reduced to the study of the mind. Then, it was questioned that since you can also not see the mind nor touch it, psychology was interpreted as a behavioral science. So, now it is basically the study of the brain and activities of the mind and how to understand or even manipulate the way the mind interacts through the body.

The downfall of this line of thinking, as far as it being true psychology, is that the brain is but living cells and the center of the nervous system. In this western approach, without the brain, the mind is dead or does not exist. But in the Vedic system that is not the case. It is described in the *Bhagavad-gita* that the mind exists outside the body and brain as a separate and subtle element, which explains the out-of- body states of being in the near-death experiences, and things like that, which is a topic by itself.

Nonetheless, Vedic "psychology" essentially means the study of the soul and its activities in the body through the nervous system, and its expression as filtered through the mind and senses. And with the insights provided in the *Bhagavad-gita*, it is also the means to become awakened to the true nature of the soul and then learn the means, through direct realization, how to act on that level of spiritual reality while still residing within the material body. Then, we overcome and solve the psychological problems of life. Without this depth of understanding, any form of real psychology remains incomplete.

ACQUIRING PROPER KNOWLEDGE

The most important thing in this life is to acquire the proper knowledge to understand the purpose of life and how to achieve it. The *Upanishads* explain that the most rare thing is to find that person who can explain to you what is the truth, in particular the Absolute Truth.

The means to acquire this is especially noted in the *Bhagavad-gita* (4.34): "Just try to learn the truth by approaching a spiritual master. Inquire from him submissively and render service unto him. The self-realized soul can impart knowledge unto you because he has seen the truth."

Submissive inquiry and rendering service is the means and etiquette to gain the favor of the spiritual teacher to impart spiritual knowledge to you. But of course, you must know how to recognize such a genuine teacher or guru. Not just anyone can call themselves a guru and be qualified for the position. And there are many fakes out there. Plus, the genuine teachers are not always so obvious, since it matters little to them how famous they are. There is an old saying that the world never knows it greatest men. In the same way, sometimes spiritual teachers are also not easily found. And the more famous such a teacher may be, the more likely they are not as genuine as you might think. So one must be careful.

However, it explains here that the self-realized soul or guru can impart spiritual knowledge to you because he is experienced. He has the direct perception of what is the Absolute and can guide you on the path so you can have the same experience. If he is not fully aware, then he may give you some advice, if he does not simply fool you in order to take advantage of you, but he may not be capable of taking you to the final goal of self-realization.

The method to understanding the truth is through guru, sadhu [holy people] and *shastra* [sacred texts]. This means to not only take instruction from a master, but to also associate with those who study and converse on such topics, along with hearing from or studying the sacred Vedic texts. Together this provides a system of checks and balances to make sure you are following the genuine path to understand the Absolute Truth and enter into the spiritual perception. As explained: "Again there are those who, although not conversant in spiritual knowledge, begin to worship the Supreme Person upon hearing about Him from others. Because of their tendency to hear from authorities, they also transcend the path of birth and death." (Bg.13.27)

This means that we may not be so qualified right now to understand the depths of this spiritual knowledge, but by reading the Vedic texts and associating with and hearing from those who are also on the path and know this information, we become qualified.

MEDITATION ACCORDING TO BHAGAVAD-GITA

Instead of spending money for courses and retreats to learn how to meditate, the *Bhagavad-gita* freely gives the authentic instructions on how to do it. It is explained in the Sixth Chapter of *Bhagavad-gita* the method of meditation, especially in the process of raja-yoga. It explains that a transcendentalist on this path of raja yoga should be free from desires, live alone, control his mind, and always concentrate on the Supreme. He should remain in a secluded and sacred place. He should arrange a seat, neither too high nor too low, with kusa-grass on the ground, covered with a soft cloth and deerskin (which was used to help keep away snakes while sitting in the forest). While sitting on the seat, the yogi should keep his body erect and stare at the tip of his nose (closing the eyes completely may lead to sleep), control the mind and senses, purify the heart, and subdue the mind to keep it unagitated and free from fear. Thus, completely free from sex life, the yogi should meditate on the Supreme as Paramatma, the Supersoul in the heart, and make Him the ultimate goal of life. By this process of controlling the body, mind, and activities, the mystic attains the spiritual strata by ending his material existence. Entering the spiritual atmosphere and achieving liberation is the ultimate level of success in this or any other form of yoga.

Naturally, setting the conditions as described may not be completely possible, so a person can more easily and simply sit on a cushion, with one's back straight, in a room or their own backyard, or wherever there are the least distractions. Then follow the next instructions as best as you can.

The yogi attains the goal of yoga after he or she

becomes situated in transcendence. This is possible only if he is temperate in his eating, sleeping, working, and recreation, and becomes devoid of all material desires. As steady as an unwavering lamp in a windless place, the yogi must meditate on the Supreme with his mind. This perfectional stage of yoga is *samadhi* or trance when the mind is free from all material engagement. The characteristic of this is that the yogi can see the self and experience boundless spiritual happiness through his transcendental senses. The yogi realizes the ultimate spiritual truth and feels nothing is greater than this. Even amidst the greatest difficulties the yogi does not give up his spiritual consciousness. Thus, he is never shaken from his position of freedom from material miseries. In this way, one should practice yoga with steady determination and abandon all varieties of material desires. Gradually, step by step, such a transcendentalist should intelligently practice yoga until he can enter the trance of thinking of nothing but the Supreme.

This description says that the meditation should be on the Supreme as the Supersoul. Therefore, we should know what is that form. According to the Vedic texts, the Supersoul is the plenary expansion of God, who is situated within the heart. How we begin to understand and perceive the Supersoul is described in *Bhagavad-gita* by Sri Krishna: "I shall now explain the knowable, knowing which you will taste the eternal. This is beginningless, and it is subordinate to Me. It is called Brahman, the spirit, and it lies beyond the cause and effect of this material world. Everywhere are His hands and legs, His eyes and faces, and He hears everything. In this way, the Supersoul exists. The Supersoul is the original source of all senses, yet He is without [material] senses. He is unattached, although He is the maintainer of all living beings. He transcends the modes of nature, and at the same time He is the master of all modes of material nature. The Supreme Truth exists both internally and externally, in the [heart of all beings] moving and nonmoving. He is beyond the power of the material senses to see or to know. Although far, far away, He is also near to all. Although the Supersoul appears to be divided, He is never divided. He is situated as one. Although He is the maintainer of every living entity, it is to be understood that He devours all and develops all. He is the source of light in all luminous objects. He is beyond the darkness of matter and is unmanifested. He is knowledge, He is the object of knowledge, and He is the goal of knowledge. He is situated in everyone's heart." (*Bg*.13.13-18)

"In this [material] body there is another, a transcendental enjoyer who is the Lord, the supreme proprietor, who exists as the overseer and permitter, and who is known as the Supersoul. That Supersoul is perceived by some through meditation [yoga], by some through the cultivation of knowledge [jnana], and by others through working without fruitive desire [no karma]. Again there are those who, although not conversant in spiritual knowledge, begin to worship the Supreme Person upon hearing about Him from others. Because of their tendency to hear from authorities, they also transcend the path of birth and death. One who sees the Supersoul accompanying the individual soul in all bodies and who understands that neither the soul nor the Supersoul is ever destroyed actually sees. One who sees the Supersoul in every living being and equal everywhere does not degrade himself by his mind. Thus, he approaches the transcendental destination." (*Bg*.13.23,25-26,28-29)

These descriptions may be hard to understand, as it describes that which is completely transcendental to the material world. Nonetheless, the Supersoul is here explained to be eternal, completely spiritual, the source of everything, yet subordinate to Lord Krishna, and expanded everywhere, dwelling within the hearts of everyone. He is the source of all light and knowledge, and the goal of all knowledge. Although the Supersoul appears to be divided by expanding in the form situated within the hearts of every living being, He is still existing as the one Absolute Truth. This is confirmed in the following verses:

"Physical nature is known to be endlessly mutable. The universe is the cosmic form of the Supreme Lord, and I [Sri Krishna] am that Lord represented as the Supersoul, dwelling in the heart of every embodied being." (*Bg*.8.4)

"The one Supreme Lord is situated within all material bodies and within everyone's soul. Just as the moon is reflected in innumerable reservoirs of water, the Supreme Lord, although one, is present within everyone. Thus, every material body is ultimately composed of the energy of the one Supreme Lord." (*Bhagavata Purana* 11.18.32)

"The Supreme Personality of Godhead has created many residential places like the bodies of human beings, animals, birds, saints, and demigods. In all these innumerable bodily forms, the Lord resides with the living beings as Paramatma [Supersoul]. Thus He is known as the *purushavatara*." (*Bhagavata Purana* 7.14.37)

"As the one sun appears reflected in countless jewels, so Govinda manifests Himself [as the Paramatma] in the hearts of all living beings." (*Caitanya-caritamrita, Adi*.2.19)

The material bodies of the living entity, although seeming to appear in different sizes and shapes, are nonetheless all made of the same basic ingredients, namely earth, air, water, etc. By understanding that within the body exists the spirit soul along with the Supersoul, there is no reason to disrespect anyone. Every living entity is spiritually part and parcel of the Supreme, and the Supreme is situated within the heart next to each of His spiritual parts and parcels. The difference is that the individual soul is situated within only one body and cannot understand what is going on in the bodies and minds of others. The Supersoul, however, is present in everyone's body and knows quite well what is happening in the minds and bodies of everyone.

How to perceive the Supersoul is through one of three ways: by perfection in meditation through which one can perceive the Supersoul (as we are describing here), or by cultivation of knowledge by which one gains the knowledge of the Supersoul, or by hearing from spiritual authorities. In any case, if one attains such spiritual vision he will actually see things as they are, and the transcendental destination then becomes achievable.

Further ways of recognizing how the Supersoul integrates the body and soul are described in the *Taittiriya Upanishad* (3.10.2). It is pointed out that one can perceive the Supersoul by the action of speech, as action in the hands, walking in the feet, and other bodily activities. In other words, it is by the power of the Supersoul within that we have the ability to do these things. This is further substantiated in *Srimad-Bhagavatam* (2.2.35) where it states: "The Personality of Godhead Lord Sri Krishna is in every living being along with the individual soul. And this fact is perceived and hypothesized in our acts of seeing and taking help from intelligence." Therefore, through the Vedic literature we can understand that the unifying factor between the desires of the self and the response of the brain and body to our desires can be recognized as the power of the Supersoul within.

The size, shape, and dress of the Supersoul, who is realized and seen by those sages who have reached the goal of knowledge through yoga, is also described in *Srimad-Bhagavatam* as follows, and is the way we should meditate on the Supersoul: "Others conceive of the Supreme Personality residing within the body in the region of the heart and measuring only eight inches, with four hands carrying a lotus, a chakra, a conchshell, and a club respectively. His mouth expresses His happiness. His eyes spread like the petals of a lotus, and His garments, yellowish like the saffron of the *kadamba* flower, are bedecked with valuable jewels. His ornaments are all made of gold, set with jewels, and He wears a glowing head-dress and earrings. His lotus feet are placed over the whorls of the lotus-like hearts of great mystics. On His chest is the Kaustubha jewel, engraved with a beautiful calf, and there are other jewels on His shoulders. His complete torso is garlanded with fresh flowers. He is well decorated with an ornamental wreath about His waist and rings studded with valuable jewels on His fingers. His leglets, His bangles, His oiled hair, curling with a bluish tint, and His beautiful smiling face are all very pleasing. The Lord's magnanimous pastimes and the glowing glancing of His smiling face are all indications of His extensive benedictions. One must therefore concentrate on this transcendental form of the Lord, as long as the mind can be fixed on Him by meditation." (Bhag.2.2.8-12)

Thus, the yogi, after being able to meditate in this way, would quit his body when he was ready, and at the proper time, and leave all material limitations behind. *Bhagavad-gita* (8.24) states that those who know the Supreme leave this world during the day, during the bright lunar fortnight, and during the six months when the sun travels to the north (summer).

In this way, the yogi who practices the raja yoga system should be so powerful that he can control when he will leave his body at the most auspicious times. Or, if a proper time is present, he should be able to raise his life air to the top of the head and, while meditating on the Supreme in devotion, immediately quit his body and enter the spiritual world. However, the *Bhagavd-gita* (8.25) states that those who leave this life during the night, the moonless fortnight, or in the six months of the southern course of the sun, or those who attain the lunar planet, again take birth in the material world. Therefore, if the yogi happened to leave his body at the improper time, or was thinking of a pleasant life in the heavenly planets, or of achieving mystical perfections, then he would not enter the spiritual world but would be transferred to the region of the universe upon which he was meditating. Or he would enter into the region where the facilities for his level of consciousness or material attachments or attractions could be best accommodated. On some of the higher material planets, in the heavenly region, the residents are born with all mystic abilities and can travel through space at will. The yogi may evolve through such higher planets lifetime after lifetime, but until the mind is pure and the consciousness spiritualized, he cannot enter into the spiritual region and will be confined to different levels of the material universe.

However, it is significant to note that even after hearing all about this system of yoga, Arjuna, who was being taught these things by Lord Krishna at the time, said that this system appears impractical and unendurable since the mind is so restless and unsteady. It is turbulent, obstinate, and very strong. To subdue it is more difficult than controlling the wind. (*Bg*.6.33-4) Therefore, we must ask if Arjuna, who was a far more capable person 5,000 years ago during the Vedic times than we are today, could perceive the difficulty of this system, then it behooves us to understand that we should expect the same challenges if we are to use this system today and hope to reach perfection with it. The ultimate stage with this form of yoga is that you are supposed to become so focused on the Supreme within and around you that you attain liberation from any further cycles of birth and death in this material creation. However, now that we are in Kali-yuga, an age of quarrel, difficulties, distractions, and discomfort, it is even harder for the majority of people to control the mind to such a degree.

Nonetheless, Lord Krishna continued to advise Arjuna that even though it is very difficult to curb the restless mind, it is possible by constant practice and detachment. "Self-realization is difficult work for one whose mind is unbridled. But My opinion is that he whose mind is controlled, and who strives by the proper process, is assured of success." (*Bg*.6.35-36)

However, Arjuna was not so convinced and still

questioned Lord Krishna. He asked what was the destination of someone who starts the process of self-realization but does not persevere, but gives up due to worldly-mindedness and does not attain success. Does such a person perish like a riven cloud, with no position anywhere? (*Bg*.6.37-38)

Here Arjuna is not merely asking about the astanga or eightfold path of yoga. He is asking about any kind of genuine process of self-realization. What happens when a sincere person still cannot reach the goal? Lord Krishna answers him that such a transcendentalist does not meet with destruction either in this world or in the next. One who does good is never overcome by evil. Even an unsuccessful yogi who cannot reach *moksha* can still reach heaven where, after many, many years of enjoyment on the heavenly planets of the pious [attained by the yogi's spiritual merit], he is born in a family of righteous people, or a wealthy family of aristocracy [due to his pious credits]. Or he takes birth in a family of transcendentalists who are already on the spiritual path and great in wisdom. Such a birth is most rare in this world. But on taking such a birth, he again revives his divine consciousness from his previous life. Then he takes up the process again and continues to make further progress in order to achieve complete success. It is by virtue of the spiritual consciousness from his previous existence that he automatically becomes attracted to the yogic principles--even without seeking them. Such an inquisitive transcendentalist, striving for yoga, stands always above the rituals prescribed in the scriptures. But when the yogi engages himself with sincere endeavor, and being washed of all contamination, then, after many, many births and deaths, he ultimately attains the supreme goal. A yogi is greater than the ascetic performing austerities, greater than the empiricist philosopher, and greater than one engaged in karmic activities for fruitive results. So, in all circumstances be a yogi. (*Bg*.6.40-46)

Herein Lord Krishna describes the positive

opportunity that awaits anyone who makes any sincere endeavor on the path of spiritual advancement, even if they do not fully succeed in one lifetime. And then He concludes in the next verse the real goal of yoga, again pointing out the ease and need for the process of bhakti yoga, loving devotion to Him. "And of all yogis, he who always abides in Me with great faith, worshiping Me in transcendental loving service [bhakti], is most intimately united with Me in yoga and is the highest of all." (*Bg*.6.47) In this way, the highest form of yoga, in Lord Krishna's opinion, is bhakti-yoga by which the yogi develops and engages in constant loving meditation and devotion to Him. This is the end goal of meditation, which is explained next.

THE SUPREME YOGA

"Therefore, Arjuna, you should always think of Me in the form of Krishna and at the same time carry out your prescribed duty. With your activities dedicated to Me and your mind and intelligence fixed on Me, you will attain Me without doubt." (Bg.8.7)

After Lord Krishna explains the process of meditation, He goes on to relate that in His view there is still something higher, and actually easier. So, now He advises that even while we are engaged in activities or duties of this world, if we stay focused and dedicated to Him, practicing the remembrance of Him and His pastimes, we will attain Him.

"A person who accepts the path of devotional service is not bereft of the results derived from studying the Vedas, performing austere practices, giving charity or pursuing philosophical and fruitive activities. At the end he reaches the supreme abode." (Bg.8.28)

Herein it is explained that because the bhakti yogi ultimately reaches the supreme abode, he or she automatically accomplishes everything else that could be achieved, whether it be through the study of Vedic knowledge or philosophical research as in jnana-yoga, or charity and work as in karma-yoga, or in breathing exercises and meditation as in raja-yoga, everything is achieved because the bhakti yogi attains the Supreme. Of course, in the process of bhakti-yoga, work is performed in loving affection for Krishna, so there is karma-yoga. Study is done to understand the qualities and pastimes of Krishna, so there is jnana-yoga. And meditation is done on Krishna's holy names and in understanding the Lord in the heart, so raja-yoga is included. But none of these processes alone can guarantee that the yogi will reach Krishna's supreme abode of Goloka Vrindavana. It is only through the attainment of the grace of Lord Krishna that the path to the supreme abode can be attained, and that is by bhakti-yoga. This is the difference. As Lord Krishna says:

"For one who worships Me, giving up all his activities unto Me and being devoted to Me without deviation, engaged in devotional service and always meditating upon Me, who has fixed his mind upon Me, O son of Pritha, for him I am the swift deliverer from the ocean of birth and death." (Bg.12.6-7)

"He who follows this imperishable path of devotional service [bhakti-yoga] and who completely engages himself with faith, making Me the supreme goal, is very, very dear to Me." (Bg.12.20)

"Always chanting My glories, endeavoring with great determination, bowing down before Me, these great souls perpetually worship Me with devotion." (Bg.9.14)

"Those who worship Me with devotion, meditating on My transcendental form–to them I carry what they lack and preserve what they have." (Bg.9.22)

This is the difference in bhakti-yoga and other forms of yoga. It is through love and devotion to Lord Krishna that spiritualizes our consciousness, but we also ask for Lord Krishna to help us. And He does. Why wouldn't He if we are sincere? There are so many stories that tell how Lord Krishna came to interact with His devotees to help propel them in their spiritual advancement. [You can see my book *Krishna Deities and Their Miracles* for many stories like this.]

So, in bhakti we ask Krishna for His blessings so we are not left alone to do what we can. But that means we have to have faith. And with that you begin the process. Then as your progress continues, you begin to get the taste for spiritual life in bhakti-yoga until you begin to perceive in so many ways the direct reciprocation from Krishna Himself, which brings His assistance to a whole new level, as Lord Krishna says next:

"Engage your mind in always thinking of Me, offer obeisances and worship Me. Being completely absorbed in Me, surely you will come to Me." (Bg.9.34)

"The Blessed Lord said: He whose mind is fixed on My personal form, always engaged in worshiping Me with great and transcendental faith, is considered by Me to be most perfect." (Bg.12.2)

Who are we trying to please? For whom do we engage in religion or any spiritual process? We do not do it merely out of curiosity. Of course, you can begin it that way, but if we are trying to enter the spiritual world or the kingdom of God, then according to *Bhagavad-gita* it is Krishna who should be pleased with our endeavor to become qualified for entering the spiritual world. Then He will pave the way and open the door. Otherwise it is not so easy. And here in the above verse He says who He considers the most perfect. Then He will help us.

In this way, by simply engaging ourselves in meditating on the Lord's personal form, and by remembering His pastimes, discussing His qualities, chanting and singing His names, is not a difficult process. When compared to other forms of yoga and disciplines, it is easy to do.

"For those whose minds are attached to the unmanifested, impersonal [Brahman] feature of the

Supreme, advancement [on this path] is very troublesome. To make progress in that discipline is always difficult for those who are embodied." (Bg.12.5)

Therefore, "This divine [material] energy of Mine, consisting of the three modes of material nature, is difficult to overcome. But those who have surrendered unto Me can easily cross beyond it." (Bg.7.14)

"This knowledge is the king of education, the most secret of all secrets. It is the purest knowledge, and because it gives direct perception of the self [soul] by realization, it is the perfection of religion. It is everlasting, and it is joyfully performed." (9.2)

In other words, the more we are focused on the Supreme Reality in this personal form of Krishna, the more our consciousness becomes fixed on Him, and the more likely we will think of Him when we leave this body at the time of death, and then attain His eternal abode. This is the easiest and most direct path to attain the Supreme. As Lord Krishna clearly says:

"Just fix your mind upon Me, the Supreme Person, and engage all your intelligence in Me. Thus you will live in Me always without a doubt." (Bg.12.8)

(For a complete step-by-step description of the process of bhakti-yoga, you can see my book "Bhakti Yoga: The Easy Path of Devotional Yoga.")

OPTIONS FOR THOSE WHO CANNOT FOLLOW THE SPIRITUAL PATH

Lord Krishna is so kind that though He establishes and explains the methods to make spiritual progress, and the path to reach the spiritual world, His supreme abode, there are those who naturally cannot or are not so inclined to take to such a direct spiritual process. Therefore, He gives some practical alternatives for the indirect methods by which a person can still make progress that can elevate him or her over the course of this lifetime.

For example, He explains, "My dear Arjuna... if you cannot fix your mind upon Me without deviation, then follow the regulated principles of bhakti-yoga. In this way, you will develop a desire to attain Me." (Bg.12.9)

This means that following such principles or practices in bhakti-yoga will certainly help purify or spiritualize the mind and consciousness and bring one to automatically become uplifted from the numerous material desires that a person has, and thus make him or her more inclined toward the spiritual goals of life, up to and including understanding the nature of Krishna Himself. It is simply a matter of following the process, which then uplifts one's consciousness. In other words, if we want to purify our mind, first we purify our activities. By following the process for purified or spiritual activities using our body and senses, then our mind and consciousness automatically start to become spiritualized. As our mind becomes spiritualized, then so do our desires and aspirations. In other words, the material desires we had gradually become less significant as we realign our goals for attaining what matters most, and that is attaining the spiritual strata.

Nonetheless, if we cannot do that, then Krishna also says, "If you cannot practice the regulations of bhakti-yoga, then just try to work for Me, because by working for Me you will come to the purified stage." (Bg.12.10)

By working for Krishna means to offer *seva*, or service with the mentality that the activity is meant to please Krishna. In this case, one is detached from doing something for one's own personal enjoyment, but the activity is meant for Krishna's enjoyment, mostly by your attitude of offering service, which is the basis of bhakti-yoga. Krishna, being God, obviously does not need anything, but we can offer Him our love by performing service to Him. This is pleasing to Him.

How do we do this? These days an easy process is simply going to the temple and volunteering various services, such as offering prayers and worship, but then helping clean the temple floors, or organize the temple for events, helping with festivals, or simply asking the temple authorities what help is needed. As you become acquainted with the temple and its administration, you can also become more familiar with what is needed and how to help, all for pleasing the deities in the temple. This is how we can advance spiritually.

Krishna still offers more alternatives if you cannot do this much: "If, however, you are not able to work in this consciousness, then act giving up all results of your work and try to be self-situated." (Bg.12.11)

In other words, try to be less attached to enjoying everything you do, and begin to curb the amount of material desires that you have. This can also be done by offering the earnings from your activities to a higher cause, like to a temple or a spiritual institution. Then you get spiritual benefit from your actions.

"If you cannot take to this practice, then engage yourself in the cultivation of knowledge. Better than knowledge, however, is meditation, and better than meditation is renunciation of the fruits of action, for by such renunciation one can attain peace of mind." (Bg.12.12)

So, here is another part of the formula, cultivation of spiritual knowledge. This is a natural part of inquiring about spiritual life, understanding the eternal spiritual truths that we, as spirit souls, are part of. This can be done by reading the *Bhagavad-gita*, which gives so much spiritual knowledge. In fact, Lord Krishna outlines the benefit of reading it, "And I declare that he who studies this sacred conversation worships Me by his intelligence." (Bg.18.70) Therefore, reading it not only gives spiritual knowledge, but it is also a form of meditation and worship of Lord Krishna. So it is beneficial on so many levels.

Furthermore, Krishna also explains, "And one who listens [or reads it] with faith and without envy becomes free from sinful reaction and attains to the [heavenly] planets where the pious dwell." (Bg.18.71)

So, it can't get much easier than that. But if you can't even do that, then Krishna says simply act in a way that gives you peace of mind, such as becoming free from so many material desires, because having peace of mind is the best mood in which to begin inquiring into spiritual topics.

BHAGAVAD-GITA AS A KEY TO SPIRITUAL ENLIGHTENMENT

One of the most important purposes of the *Bhagavad-gita* is that it is a primary key to spiritual enlightenment. It is said to deliver the essential knowledge of the *Upanishads* in one book. So, it is good for people who may not have a lot of time for reading. It also presents spiritual information more clearly than what may be found elsewhere, besides containing many instructions directly from Lord Krishna.

In this way, by utilizing the knowledge in the *Bhagavad-gita*, we can begin to understand what is our true identity as a spiritual being who is presently encased in a material machine or body, and learn how to recognize our situation. This certainly separates those with knowledge from the foolish, as stated by Lord Krishna in the following verses:

"Some look on the soul as amazing, some describe him as amazing, and some hear of him as amazing, while others, even after hearing about him, cannot understand him at all." (Bg.2.29)

"The foolish cannot understand how a living entity can quit his body, nor can they understand what sort of body he enjoys under the spell of the modes of nature. But one whose eyes are trained [opened] in knowledge can see all this. The endeavoring transcendentalist, who is situated in self-realization, can see all this clearly. But those who are not situated in self-realization cannot see what is taking place, though they may try to." (Bg.15.10-11)

For those who have no spiritual vision, they will never understand the ways of spiritual reality. However, after we begin to study and comprehend this knowledge, we start to see through the eyes of wisdom. Then we can see the reality of our circumstances, beyond the temporary appearances of the ever-changing material energy and the many forms it presents that keep us preoccupied with it. An example of such a view of reality, when we can recognize the spiritual reality around us, is described in the following verses:

"One who sees the Supersoul accompanying the individual soul in all bodies and who understands that neither the soul nor the Supersoul is ever destroyed, actually sees." (Bg.13.28)

This describes the eternal nature of the soul, which is accompanied by the Lord's local expansion of Supersoul, who is the companion of each and every soul in every situation we may encounter. This shows that though we may abandon God at certain times, He never abandons us. The next verses go a little deeper in explaining the nature of the soul and the spiritual vision we should have.

"One who can see that all activities are performed by the body, which is created of material nature, and sees that the self does nothing, actually sees." (Bg.13.30)

"When a sensible man ceases to see different identities, which are due to different material bodies, he attains to the Brahman [spiritual] conception. Thus he sees that beings are expanded everywhere." (Bg.13.31)

"Those with the vision of eternity can see that the soul is transcendental, eternal, and beyond the modes of nature. Despite contact with the material body, O Arjuna, the soul neither does anything nor is entangled." (Bg.13.32)

"The sky, due to its subtle nature, does not mix with anything, although it is all-pervading. Similarly, the soul, situated in Brahman vision, does not mix with the body, though situated in that body." (Bg.13.33)

These verses describe how the soul may be in a material body but is always separate from it, though interacting through it. No spiritual path is complete unless it can give instructions that enable the conditioned soul to become free once and for all of being entrapped in this material body and existence.

"O son of Bharata, as the sun alone illuminates all this universe, so does the living entity, one within the body, illuminate the entire body by consciousness." (Bg.13.34)

Herein, this verse explains that the evidence for the soul within the body is the consciousness that pervades the body. Just like if you pinch anywhere on the body, whether it be a human body or an animal body, there will be pain. The natural impulse is to avoid that pain. That is the sign of consciousness, which is exhibited by the instinct to survive. Even plants act in ways to get enough sunlight and water. That also is the evidence of the presence of a soul within that body. When we recognize this, we begin to recognize how there is life everywhere and the soul exists in all kinds of bodies. This knowledge helps propel a person to the spiritual dimension, as the next verse describes:

"One who knowingly sees this difference between the body and the owner of the body [the soul] and can understand the process of liberation from bondage, also attains the supreme goal." (Bg.13.35)

These verses may require some contemplation, but when understood can certainly provide a view of how to see the world and the way we fit into it. It is through this spiritual knowledge that we can acquire the means to see things as they are. But we need to do more than merely see our situation. We also need to attain the supreme goal or spiritual abode. In other words, we need to become free from being trapped in the material elements.

It is not only through the study of such Vedic texts like the *Bhagavad-gita*, but as Lord Krishna has stated, there must also be the practice of the methods that are recommended, specifically and most easily through the process of bhakti-yoga or devotional service to Lord Krishna. This also purifies and then spiritualizes our consciousness so that we can actually realize and then perceive this level of reality that exists all around us. Then we live in this awareness and also engage in the process of bhakti-yoga. This is the true goal of human life, without which we will have to keep trying in other lifetimes. The choice is up to us. But herein Lord Krishna advises us of the importance of using this life and opportunity appropriately for our spiritual development:

"That is the way of the spiritual and godly life, after attaining which a person is not bewildered. Being so situated, even at the hour of death, one can enter into the kingdom of God." (Bg.2.72)

BHAGAVAD-GITA AND ESTABLISHING WORLD PEACE

If we have read all the material so far about developing ourselves spiritually, we should be able to recognize that this nonsectarian information about the soul and how to act within the material world, we should also understand how this should promote genuine peace around the planet. Whether it be through the means of being a good manager, or the qualities in good work ethics, or recognizing the soul within all others, and the means of dealing with stress or controlling the mind, or in understanding how everyone is a part of God, this should instill in us the proper mentality to not only be at peace, but to treat others in a spiritual manner.

This does not mean we treat others with respect only if they fit a certain criteria, or are like us, but we have to change our vision so that we understand how to see all others in the proper light, the light of spiritual awareness.

By following the principles as set by the *Bhagavad-gita* as we have been presenting, there should be no reason why we should not be able to use these same principles to establish world peace. It's all a matter of how we utilize this information.

* * *

    These are just some of the examples that we can find in the *Bhagavad-gita* on how it can be used in addressing challenges in modern life. There are many more that can be found, and many other writers, teachers and gurus have written about them. But these should be enough to give the impetus for the reader of this book to acquire their own copy of the *Bhagavad-gita* and give it serious study for their own benefit. There is much that can be found within it, and it often speaks to you in a personal way that may affect you in the manner best for you.

    The next chapter will continue to provide further insights for your own spiritual development and present the qualities and means to acquire them that will help you make the most progress. In this way, the *Bhagavad-gita* has much to offer.

CHAPTER THREE

Thirty-one Days to Liberation on the Vedic Path

This chapter is based on the 108 most essential verses of the *Bhagavad-gita* and clearly helps show how easy and simple this path can be. By taking one lesson a day and adding the recommended principles and characteristics to your life, by the end of 31 days, as long as you do not give up the spiritual principles you have accepted, you will have most everything you need to reach *moksha*, as it is called in Sanskrit, which means liberation from material existence through enlightenment. That is the main point: do not give up the spiritual assets that you have acquired for spiritual liberation through these instructions. This chapter is meant for the advancement of Santana-dharma, the eternal and universal spiritual path meant for everyone.

INTRODUCTION

Some of the greatest spiritual books in the world and deepest spiritual instructions are those in the Vedic literature. And the essence of the Vedic path, which many also call Hinduism, are the *Upanishads*, the *Vedanta Sutras*, and especially the *Bhagavad-gita*. The *Bhagavad-*

gita contains the most important teachings of Lord Krishna and the foundation of Vedic wisdom. Therefore, we will take some of the essential verses from the *Bhagavad-gita* and show a 31-day course of action that leads to *moksha*. This means liberation from material existence which takes us back to the Kingdom of God. This path is for anyone, and will certainly lead you to a new and exciting life.

As you proceed through this chapter, you will see how God is your friend who cares about you and wants you to understand this knowledge about your spiritual identity and your eternal, loving relationship with Him.

Sometimes in this world you may have felt hopeless, depressed, or overwhelmed with the sorrow that is often seen in this troubled land, or even unsure of yourself and what path you should take. But God wants you to rise up out of that mindset of darkness and come back to Him. And you can do that in this life, right now. In understanding and pursuing the Vedic path of spirituality, I wanted to show how simple yet deep and profound it can be. So this will help inspire and guide you through a progressive month of reflection and advancement to spiritual liberation.

By following these simple instructions for the next 31 days, one lesson each day, you will be relieved of so much confusion about life and will attain a high level of peace and clarity. You will see that reaching God is not difficult. This can and will change your life. It is simple, easy, and requires no money. You can do it alone, or with friends and family. Reviving your connection with the loving God Krishna will be a most fulfilling experience. It can fill the emptiness in your life.

Lord Krishna has always been your friend, waiting for you to turn toward Him. And now is your chance to reawaken your awareness of your true spiritual nature and how you are always connected with Him. This is your destiny. This is what your life was meant for. And now is your chance to open the door to that rare and special destiny. This is God's message to you just as He spoke this message to Arjuna, another friend of His in the *Bhagavad-gita*. You simply have to be open to the message.

Use these verses to start your daily morning meditations or prayers, or quiet times of reflection. Take a day to contemplate each point and to make the necessary change for spiritual progress. This does not mean that merely by reading this you will attain liberation, but if you add the attributes or activities that are suggested in these verses, and seriously keep them in your life and continue practicing them, then by the time you finish this course you will have most everything you need to attain *moksha*. Also, get a copy of the *Bhagavad-gita*, if you do not already have one, to continue your studies and spiritual advancement. Use this booklet as often as you want for introspection on yourself and to see how far you have progressed, or to continue your steady advancement toward liberation from material existence and your attainment of the spiritual world. You will see that the spiritual strata is much closer than you think.

DAY ONE: BEGINNING YOUR NEW LIFE

"In this endeavor there is no loss or diminution, and a little advancement on this path can protect one from the most dangerous type of fear." (Bg.2.40)

* * *

One of the most important things to understand is that a little progress on the spiritual path is eternal. It stays with you forever. It is not like material or bodily development that lasts a short time, or, if you're lucky, as long as you keep your body. For example, you may work so hard saving money for a nice vacation, but however pleasant or adventurous your trip may be, your money will be spent afterwards and when you return you will have to start saving your money again.

Or you may study for a great career, and even get started working in the field of your choice, only to find that as the world changes, your occupation is no longer needed so much. Or you get laid off from your job. Then you have to start something new.

Or you may have had a most pleasant life, surrounded by wife and family, living in a beautiful house and so on, but then the time comes when you get old and sickly and then you die, forcing you to leave everything you had. No one wants this, but this is the nature of material existence, where change is the only constant, whether it is wanted or not. It is forced on you.

However, whatever spiritual advancement you make never dwindles, nor changes or becomes lost. Even if you make only a little advancement in your life, it stays with you to be picked up and added to in your next life. Plus, it will naturally keep you moving forward lifetime after lifetime. That way after death you will not enter any dark areas or hellish situations. You are protected. And where we go after death is a foremost concern of many people as they get old and decrepit. But no such fear need exist for one who follows this spiritual path.

DAY TWO: WHY BE ABSORBED IN GOD?

"Being freed from attachment, fear and anger, being fully absorbed in Me and taking refuge in Me, many, many persons in the past became purified by knowledge of Me–and thus they all attained transcendental love for Me." (Bg.4.10)

* * *

While beginning the path of spiritual knowledge, a person may wonder what is so special about it. Why try to be absorbed in God? Does it actually work? But herein Lord Krishna explains that this process is not new. There have been numerous persons in the past who have been successful. Of course, we may hear of the acharyas and spiritual teachers who have attained success and who have provided their teachings for others. But there are so many simple people who have been successful and returned to the spiritual domain that we have never heard of at all. And you may be next.

So we should have no doubt that if we really want to attain success on the path, this process of genuine spiritual knowledge and devotion to God is the easiest and most direct, which will be explained further as we move through this course. This knowledge and process will help you to understand God. By such insights and realizations many, many people have attained such spiritual fortune. Therefore, we need to pick up our enthusiasm to move forward knowing that we are following a path that many others have already traveled to the ultimate success in life.

DAY THREE: HAVE FAITH AND KEEP WALKING IN THE LIGHT

"But ignorant and faithless persons who doubt the revealed scriptures do not attain God consciousness. For the doubting soul there is happiness neither in this world nor in the next." (Bg.4.40)

* * *

The start of something new always requires faith, no matter whether it is starting a new job, moving to a new location, getting married, etc. We have to have faith that it will work to our benefit. But in this case we know that by pursuing the spiritual path, it will make positive differences and improvements in our life, in our consciousness, and even in the world. This is the long-term goal and award-- attaining God consciousness.

Of course, as it is said in the above verse, for those who have no faith and who doubt the advice in words of God in the revealed scriptures attain neither God consciousness nor real happiness. The point is that happiness itself must come from within. There is no external or bodily activity that will bring happiness if you do not already have some joy in your heart. Naturally, some bodily activities may bring some pleasure, excitement or thrills, but they will not invoke a deep feeling of fulfillment if they do not affect you on a higher spiritual level. In fact, most bodily acts simply give you something to do while time slips away. They are like diversionary tactics that keep your mind and body occupied while time goes by.

Naturally, we do have to expect that there will be those who doubt the revealed scriptures or the instructions of God. But we have to look at them with sympathy because experience has shown many times that individuals who are dedicated to that which gives little else but temporary pleasure are often left with feeling less than fulfilled. They may even be disappointed, cynical or even lost in life, though they may not admit it. So we do not want to take such a road.

However, while traveling and walking in the light of spiritual awareness means that whatever you do will bring higher and deeper levels of joy and happiness. As we continue to walk the spiritual path, everything will get clearer. The point is that beauty and happiness are already within you. You are a creation of the source of all beauty and joy. The spiritual path merely reveals the inner and spiritual you, and relieves you of the mistake of identifying with the excess complications or illusory drama that goes on around us. This sort of experience increases our faith since it is the result of our dedication and witnessing what can happen in our own life by taking these instructions seriously.

DAY FOUR: TRANSCENDENTAL KNOWLEDGE, THE WAY TO PEACE AND CLARITY

"In this world, there is nothing so sublime and pure

as transcendental knowledge. Such knowledge is the mature fruit of all mysticism. And one who has achieved this enjoys the self within himself in due course of time." (Bg.4.38)

"The sages, knowing Me as the ultimate purpose of all sacrifices and austerities, the Supreme Lord of all planets and demigods, and the benefactor and well-wisher of all living entities, attain peace from the pangs of material miseries." (Bg.5.29)

* * *

Knowledge is the essence of power, the motivator for change and development. And spiritual knowledge is from the power of light. It can put you in touch with your higher Self up to the point of perceiving the existence of the Supreme, if used properly.

Knowledge is also the awareness of the purpose of life. And the above verses point out that the wise sages who know that the ultimate purpose is to understand our spiritual identity and God, attain the supreme peace, and engage all their activities for progressing toward that goal. This is to uncover ourselves from the illusion or maya, which hides the reality of our spiritual essence. This is one of the main things that spiritual knowledge can do for us.

Therefore, following in the footsteps of the sages, we can enter the sublime peace by utilizing transcendental knowledge to perceive our real self and to understand the ultimate goal of life. Then we can enjoy our higher selves that are within this body, and deeper than the mind, and eternally connected with the Supreme Being. This perception is what actually reveals the true purpose of human existence and brings peace from the complexities of material life.

This is the importance of cultivating our understanding of transcendental knowledge and its difference from material knowledge and education. Real education is not merely a matter of gaining some craft or skill, like becoming an artist, or car mechanic, or even a doctor or computer technician. Real education is that which unveils who we are and what is the spiritual dimension. This is what shows how this material life of ours is only a lightning flash when compared to the eternality of our soul's existence. That is what we need to perceive. That is why it is said:

"This knowledge is the king of education, the most secret of all secrets. It is the purest knowledge, and because it gives direct perception of the self by realization, it is the perfection of religion. It is everlasting, and it is joyfully performed." (Bg.9.2)

DAY FIVE: WHY THIS KNOWLEDGE IS GIVEN TO YOU

"This very ancient science of the relationship with the Supreme is today told by Me to you because you are My devotee as well as My friend; therefore you can understand the transcendental mystery of this science." (Bg.4.3)

* * *

One thing for sure is that if you are here reading this, you are alive. And if you are alive, then you are here for a purpose. You are special. You are not an accident. You are a spiritual being in a material body. You are a product of God's intention. You are a spiritual part of God and have every chance of regaining that awareness and realization. When we raise our awareness above the level of ordinary activities, free from mental and sensual influences, then we can get a glimpse of that reality which makes it clear that we are spiritual in nature, above all the mundane things that go on all around us. The reality is that you are actually connected directly to God, if you can only be aware of it.

Furthermore, as a spiritual being, you are always connected with God. That never changes. You only need to fully awaken this awareness to understand the comfort and loving exchange that is possible between you and God. And God provides full facility for the living beings to awaken to this awareness by providing books that contain His message, such as *Bhagavad-gita*, or gurus and teachers who can show the way. The Lord can also provide you the impetus to search out this knowledge by providing inspiration from within, as the Supersoul.

In any case, God is your friend. He is concerned for you, and that is why you are being presented with this knowledge. It is all God's arrangement for your upliftment. If you use this properly, the reciprocation between you and God will increase. Your relationship with God will become more apparent and your natural position as God's devotee will be revealed, and the transcendental mystery will become unveiled. Therefore, it is God's concern for you that you now have been given this opportunity.

DAY SIX: LEARNING SPIRITUAL TRUTH GIVES PROPER UNDERSTANDING

"And when you have thus learned the truth, you will know that all living beings are but part of Me–that they are in Me, and are mine." (Bg.4.35)

* * *

As you continue with this path of devotion to God and your study of His instructions, not only will your own relationship with God be rekindled and gradually revealed, but you will also see how all other entities are also spiritual beings, though forgetful of this since they are in varieties of material species of life. And the human form provides the best facility in the way of intelligence to analyze and discern our spiritual identity. And since all creatures are also spiritual in essence, they are also parts and parcels of God. They all belong to God. In fact, everything is but a display of the energy of God. In this consciousness you will see that actually God is everywhere. What is not God? Thus, you will never feel alone because all beings are parts of God and all things are but the energy of God.

Furthermore, in this vision of spiritual truth you will see how everything is balanced. The material creation comes from an initial cause, which comes from God. And everything that happens to us is also based on the process of actions and reactions, or cause and effect. This is called the law of karma. Thus, nothing happens without a reason.

Yet, those who are without such a spiritual perception cannot understand all this. In fact, they may challenge or even insult the spiritual perspective. Thus, they are affected by and remain stuck in their own foolishness. In this way, they stay helpless to do anything but put all their energy into making the most of this one life because this is all they see. Plus, they are ignorant of what lies beyond. That is why Lord Krishna explains:

"The endeavoring transcendentalist, who is situated in self-realization, can see all this clearly. But those who are not situated in self-realization cannot see what is taking place, though they may try to." (Bg.15.11)

DAY SEVEN: FOLLOW THE PURPOSE OF LIFE

"The yogis, abandoning attachment, act with body, mind, intelligence, and even with the senses, only for the purpose of purification." (Bg.5.11)

* * *

As you progress in your spiritual purification and realizations, you will see how to use all aspects of your life toward your spiritual progress. So from the time you get up, to taking care of your children and family, or going to work, dealing with others, even eating and sleeping, can all be done in a way that adds to your spiritual development. All activities can provide lessons to learn and give insights into our connection with God and all His parts and parcels.

Or it may also give insights into the futility of pursuing sensual delights which will emphasize the need to continue our spiritual advancement. In this way, we will remain motivated to use the body like a tool, along with the mind and intelligence, for purification in our transcendental existence.

By acting in this manner, for the real purpose of life, we will continue to have deeper and deeper realizations. As we develop, then in the not far too distant future, we will be assured of liberation from mundane vision and material existence, and return to the kingdom of God. As Lord Krishna describes:

"Those who are free from anger and all material desires, who are self-realized, self-disciplined and constantly endeavoring for perfection, are assured of liberation in the Supreme in the very near future." (Bg.5.26)

DAY EIGHT: BE DILIGENT ON THE PATH

"From whatever and wherever the mind wanders due to its flickering and unsteady nature, one must certainly withdraw it and bring it back under the control of the Self. The yogi whose mind is fixed on Me verily attains the highest happiness. By virtue of his identity with Brahman, he is liberated; his mind is peaceful, his passions are quieted, and he is freed from sin." (Bg.6.26-27)

* * *

Naturally, treading the spiritual path may not always be easy. We have been so conditioned to the material lifestyle that there may be times when we must tolerate the unnecessary urges of the senses, or suffer the mood swings of the mind, or even be exposed to demands and wants of others around us. All these may affect us in certain ways, or make us consider compromising our spiritual standards, regulations or practice as they pull us this way or that. But we must simply keep trying and never give up. It's as simple as that. When we see ourselves getting off-track, we simply pull ourselves back. When our mind wanders off in the wrong direction, then we must use the intelligence and pull it back where it belongs.

We should never get discouraged and never get depressed or think that the process will not work. There are already so many others who have succeeded before us. You must simply step back and witness how the material energy works, or how the mind reacts to various situations. Then remember how you are the spirit and not the mind. So you have to keep working at controlling the mind, which merely takes practice over the long-term. How well you control the mind indicates how much you are advancing. In time, with spiritual advancement, the mind will not be so restless or attracted to materialistic activities. It will simply lose interest.

So how you control the mind is simply how you engage it. The more you read the spiritual and Vedic books, or associate with others to discuss spiritual topics and the activities of God, or meditate and chant God's holy names, the more of a positive impact they will make on the mind. Then the more purified it becomes, and, naturally, our lives become more peaceful. As we become freer from bodily attachment, we are also less attracted to questionable or debilitating desires, habits and activities. This is what paves the way for our mind to remain fixed on God, without swings and shifts, and attain the greatest happiness.

DAY NINE: KEEP ADDING HIGHER QUALITIES TO YOUR CHARACTER

"Humility, pridelessness, nonviolence, tolerance, simplicity, approaching a genuine spiritual master, cleanliness, steadiness and self-control; renunciation of the objects of sense gratification, absence of false ego, the perception of the evil of birth, death, old age and disease;

nonattachment to children, wife, home and the rest, and even-mindedness amid pleasant and unpleasant events; constant and unalloyed devotion to Me, resorting to solitary places, detachment from the general mass of people; accepting the importance of self-realization, and philosophical search for the Absolute Truth–all these I thus declare to be knowledge, and what is contrary to these is ignorance." (Bg.13.8-12)

* * *

We must always be aware of the need for constant improvement in our character, and for adding qualities that serve our purpose. The above verses list a number of such qualities that we need to consider and see how best we can add them to our character.

To sum up a few of these, humility is to see ourselves as spiritual sparks that are no different than any other of the innumerable souls spread throughout the creation. This leads to loss of pride, tolerance of any situation, and following a simple lifestyle. Nonviolence means to be kind and understanding in body, mind and words. Ultimately nonviolence means to relieve people of their suffering by giving them spiritual knowledge so they can rise above the bodily platform. This also leads to the renunciation of objects for gratifying the senses. Cleanliness is next to godliness, as it is said. So we should strive to be clean in both body and mind.

False ego means to identify with the temporary body, which is not our real self. Absence of false ego means to see yourself as the spirit soul that merely occupies the body, like being in a container, or the driver of a vehicle. Then all forms of bodily distinctions, whether it is beauty, intelligence, strength, riches, etc., will not weigh us down with false ego and pride.

Perception of the evil in birth, death, old age and disease means to recognize the disturbance or unnaturalness that this causes for us. We naturally have goals, but this cycle of birth and death disrupts everything and is the opposite of our eternal nature. Nonattachment to our children, wife, home and the rest means to recognize that though you may interact with them and have responsibilities for them, nonetheless they belong to God. They are not entirely yours but have been given by God and actually belong to God. So you have to act in a godly way in your concern and love for them, and train them in God-consciousness as well. If you are married or have children, you must accept those responsibilities. Nonattachment does not mean that you use spiritual life as an excuse to give up your responsibilities to your dependents. That would be the exact opposite to what is spiritual life. Spiritual life means you become the most responsible. Seeing your family and possessions in the right frame of mind leads you to even-mindedness amid pleasant and unpleasant events. This is necessary.

    This is what leads to constant and unalloyed devotion to God, and the desire to remain in a situation, whether it is solitary places or remaining aloof from the materialistic mass of society, wherein it is most accommodating for continuing your process of self-realization. All of these qualities is what Krishna declares to be knowledge, which is uplifting. Contrary to these principles is darkness, which drags one further into ignorance and the continuation of one's material existence. As Lord Krishna says:

    "Fearlessness, purification of one's existence, cultivation of spiritual knowledge. Charity, self-control, performance of sacrifice, study of the Vedas, austerity and simplicity; nonviolence, truthfulness, freedom from anger; renunciation, tranquility, aversion to faultfinding, compassion and freedom from covetousness; gentleness, modesty and steady determination; vigor, forgiveness, fortitude, cleanliness, freedom from envy and the passion for honor–these transcendental qualities, O son of Bharata, belong to godly men endowed with divine nature." (Bg.16.1-3)

DAY TEN: ACCEPT A PROPER SPIRITUAL TEACHER

"Just try to learn the truth by approaching a spiritual master. Inquire from him submissively and render service unto him. The self-realized soul can impart knowledge unto you because he has seen the truth." (Bg.4.34)

* * *

One thing we need to understand is that to make sure we are always going in the right direction, or whenever we have questions, or when there are problems to sort out while traveling the spiritual road, it is not always enough to depend on a book. But you need a spiritual teacher, a guru whom you can approach for guidance. A genuine guru can help in making sure we remain on the right path.

Sometimes people feel there is no need for a guru. But in this material world, we are all born in varying degrees of darkness. It takes a spiritual teacher to pull us out of the illusion. And no matter how a person acquires spiritual knowledge, whether it is through this book, or through a friend or some other way, it can all be traced back to a spiritual teacher somewhere. So accepting a proper guru or teacher is important. Only by being humble enough to accept spiritual knowledge from without can we become qualified to receive such knowledge from within.

A guru is one who should be in a proper sampradaya or chain of disciplic succession, and his teachings must also be in accordance with what the scripture verifies, and with what other advanced *sadhus* or devotees teach. This is the unique system of checks and balances that is used in the Vedic system. It is not that just anyone can claim to be a guru and say anything he likes. But the guru, scripture and sages must all corroborate each other to make sure people are not fooled or improperly instructed. If a guru says something that is not established in scripture, or is not advocated or approved by other knowledgeable sages, then his authority may be called into question. So following these checks a person can verify that he is following rightly.

Once a proper teacher is found, then you must approach him submissively. You cannot order him to give spiritual knowledge, which is rare to find anyway. In exchange for the guidance and instruction, traditionally it is expected that you offer some service in exchange, or some *dakshina*, which is an offering of money. This also purifies the time you spent making the money that is offered. A spiritually realized and experienced guru can guide you because he is accepting you to follow in his footsteps to the same spiritual reality that he has already entered. However, one needs to be careful because such a soul is very rare, and if we might find such a person, we should take it most seriously. As Lord Krishna explains:

"Out of many thousands among men, one may endeavor for perfection, and of those who have achieved perfection, hardly one knows Me in truth." (Bg.7.3)

DAY ELEVEN: ADJUSTING YOUR DIET FOR HIGHER AWARENESS

"If one offers Me with love and devotion a leaf, a flower, fruit or water, I will accept it." (Bg.9.26)

* * *

This verse shows a few things. First it shows how simple the worship of God can be. Often times it seems expected that Vedic or Hindu rituals cost much money, especially those performed in the temples. Sometimes when we visit certain temples in India the priests try to force us into engaging in a ritual and then ask for a large offering of money, *dakshina*. However, we should not feel forced to make extravagant offerings or pay a priest large amounts of money if we have no such facility. Devotional service is not meant to be a business, but a means of offering our love to God. Without that even the most opulent offerings do not gain much favor in the eyes of God. If we have much love and devotion, that is the biggest asset even if our offering is simple. Such a modest offering filled with love and devotion is more than acceptable to Lord Krishna.

So, we can certainly worship God by going to the temple, seeing the Deity, saying our prayers, and provide a little offering according to our capacity. Or we may simply have a Deity or a picture or symbol at home and offer a little something there. Of course, if we do have plenty of funds, then we can even help build a temple if we want, or sponsor a huge festival or something else. The point is that it must be a sign of our love and devotion to be accepted.

The second thing this verse shows is that God asks for items which cause no harm to others. He asks for no blood offerings or for the meat of slaughtered animals. Thus, as He outlines here, we offer nice flowers, fruits, grains, or sumptuous vegetable preparations. Similarly, after the items are offered, we accept the remnants of such offerings as *prasada*, known as His mercy on us. Because we partake of such sacred food that has been offered to God, we also make great spiritual advancement. The *prasada* purifies our minds and bodies.

There have already been experiments that show how praying over food will subtly change its molecular structure in a positive way. So when we prepare food in the proper consciousness, with the intent of offering it to God, in the form of His Deity or picture, with prayers and worship, then we can imagine how much more the food changes and becomes purified.

Furthermore, if we are serious about making spiritual advancement, we do not want to put things in our body which depletes our energy, our health, or lowers our vibration, thoughts and consciousness. So a few things that will do that are tobacco, intoxicants like drugs or alcohol, as well as meat. Meat is a product of violence since the animal has to be killed. No entity wants to be killed. So this kind of violence enters your system when you eat the meat. It lowers your consciousness and sensitivity to the point where you may no longer perceive anything wrong with killing the lives of animals so you can satisfy your tongue. This, of course, does not take into consideration how many drugs are put into the bodies of livestock which are bred to be butchered, nor the conditions in which they are slaughtered. But if you are sincere about raising your own consciousness, and keeping yourself free from the karma of contributing to the violence of unnecessary killing, then you should consider these points and adjust your intake of foods accordingly and at least take to the vegetarian diet. In other words, we do not want to cause harm to others or ourselves, so we do not partake in eating things that will do that, or that will cause resistance to our spiritual progress. And the meat diet is not difficult to give up when we have experienced the higher taste of what can be done with delicious vegetable preparations.

DAY TWELVE: YOU ARE NOT YOUR BODY

"Those with the vision of eternity can see that the soul is transcendental, eternal, and beyond the modes of nature. Despite contact with the material body, O Arjuna, the soul neither does anything nor is entangled." (Bg.13.32)

* * *

In spiritual training, perhaps the single most important point to understand is that you are not your body. You are the soul within it. The soul is completely transcendental to the body, and does not come under the same designations that we give to the body. It does not belong to a certain family name or ethnic group. The soul is not Hindu, Christian, Muslim, Jewish, etc. It is also not American, Indian, Russian, Chinese, Pakistani, or anything else. According to the Upanishads it is also not happy, sad, frustrated or content, nor does it imagine anything but what it ought to imagine. It does not take birth, grow, change or die. It may be in the body, and we may think we are the body due to false ego, but we have the freedom to think whatever we like.

There is a saying that anything that is temporary or changes is not the eternal truth. We have to go beyond what is temporary to get a glimpse of what is real and true. And the soul exists in that field of eternity that is completely beyond the mind, body and senses.

Only with genuine spiritual vision can we see our real identity, beyond the body, beyond all of material nature. The soul is never entangled in the material energy or actions, nor does it engage in such. It is only the body and our bodily desires which keep us bound up in material nature. It is only by thinking we are these bodies which keeps us in the bodily existence. This is why it is so important to pursue spiritual life and rise above the mental and bodily dictates that limit our perception of our spiritual identity. That is where we can reach our full potential, beyond the limitations that are forced on us by our absorption in material existence. The more spiritual we become, the more we can perceive the spiritual level of reality.

DAY THIRTEEN: YOU ARE ETERNAL

The Blessed Lord said: "While speaking learned words, you are mourning for what is not worthy of grief. Those who are wise lament neither for the living nor the dead. Never was there a time when I did not exist, nor you, nor all these kings; nor in the future shall any of us cease to be." (Bg.2.11-12)

"For the soul there is never birth nor death. Nor, having once been, does he ever cease to be. He is unborn, eternal, ever-existing, undying and primeval. He is not slain when the body is slain." (Bg.2.20)

* * *

Once we truly understand that we, as spirit souls, are eternal, our whole attitude changes. Death can be a great fear for many individuals, but death is only a change of bodies, like a change of clothes. The soul never dies, so there is also no need to unnecessarily lament or grieve for those who have died. Naturally we may miss them but they have gone elsewhere just as we will when our time comes.

If we are spiritually prepared, then there will be nothing to fear from death. Actually, for those advanced souls, they can rise above the body enough to where they can actually perceive what lies beyond death. They can see it. Thus, they know where they will go, according to their level of consciousness. It is like dying now but leaving later. So there is nothing to fear. This is one of the goals of human life, if a person can do it.

So the point to understand is that we are eternal and that birth and death are only appearances on the material plane. Like an actor who enters a stage and plays a part in a costume until it is time to exit the stage and be reminded of who we really are. Ultimately, since we are already eternal beings, entering that spiritual dimension is the real goal of life.

DAY FOURTEEN: BECOMING FREE FROM BODILY DESIRES

"The nonpermanent appearance of happiness and distress, and their disappearance in due course, are like the appearance and disappearance of winter and summer seasons. They arise from sense perception and one must learn to tolerate them without being disturbed." (Bg.2.14)

"Before giving up this present body, if one is able to tolerate the urges of the material senses and check the force of desire and anger, he is a yogi and is happy in this world." (Bg.5.23)

* * *

Once we understand our eternal nature, which is beyond the body, we should become decreasingly influenced or motivated by bodily desires. Such desires and the pleasures we want to attain for the body are themselves temporary. They have a beginning and an end. Thus, happiness of this sort comes and goes, like the winter and summer seasons. If you don't like the weather, wait a while and it will change. Similarly, no matter whether you are happy or sad, in due time it will change. It is automatic. Sadness is followed by happiness which may again be followed by moments of sadness. Material nature provides the changes that make this happen.

However, such changes are recognized through the mind's interpretation of them. The senses detect various sensations and the mind judges whether it is agreeable or not. Then the mind develops certain moods based on the external conditions with which it is dealing. That is why this is called the mental platform.

As we can see, a person who is engaged in chasing after all their desires is often preoccupied with the superficialities of life. Like a drug addict always chasing after his next high, he is completely obsessed with it and so much of his endeavor is wasted for such temporary thrills. He gets no rest. So much time, energy and money is spent, and he is still not truly happy, though he may feel satisfied for only short periods of time.

In the same way, a person chasing after material desires or ways to satisfy the mind and senses loses so much energy and time, yet remains absorbed in the anticipation and hope for finding happiness, but in the guise of sensual or mental pleasure. This is not real contentment or fulfillment. Thus, genuine happiness eludes such a person. This is why it is said that, in order to be happy, it is better for a person to tolerate the dictates of the senses rather than giving into all of them. It is like the ocean that receives the waters from so many rivers, yet remains steady in spite of so much input.

One problem with trying to please the mind is that the mental platform is very flickering, and the mood of the mind is always changing. In other words, what was satisfying at one moment becomes boring or distasteful later. So the mind is always changing its wants. And the more you give it, the more it hankers. The more it will tell you how much it needs. Lust is a relentless master. It is like a fire being fed with gasoline. The more you feed it, the more it will consume.

So, the point is that as we become free from the bodily conception of life by knowing we are actually the eternal soul within this temporary body, we will also become free from the bodily influence and sensual or mental urges and desires. The more we can do that, the more we can be happy in this world, and the easier it will be for our spiritual pursuits.

DAY FIFTEEN: ATTAINING SPIRITUAL CONSCIOUSNESS

"A person in divine consciousness, although engaged in seeing, hearing, touching, smelling, eating, moving about, sleeping, and breathing, always knows within himself that he actually does nothing at all. Because while speaking, evacuating, receiving, opening or closing his eyes, he always knows that only the material senses are engaged with their objects and that he is aloof from them." (Bg.5.8-9)

"The humble sage, by virtue of true knowledge, sees with equal vision a learned and gentle brahmana, a cow, an elephant, a dog and a dog-eater [outcaste]." (Bg.5.18)

* * *

Here is a description of one who has attained divine consciousness. Such a person knows he or she is a spirit soul within the body. In divine consciousness you do not just know it but you can see it. You can see how your body performs so many actions, but you, as a spiritual being, are still different from those activities.

Without divine consciousness, people often forget that they are spiritual beings and think their real identity is the body. With that state of mind, they become quite enthused and motivated to give pleasure and all kinds of care to the body. That becomes their primary goal in life. But that also brings fear when they get older and closer to death. What will they do then? What will they do when they lose their possessions and that which gives their mind and senses the most pleasure? What will be their reasons for living then?

Yet those in divine consciousness can see that the body is merely a vehicle in which we are riding. And not only are we spiritual beings covered in material forms, but so are all the other living entities in this material world. Thus, such a person can see that a sophisticated human being, or a cow, an elephant, or cats and dogs, birds, insects, plants, etc., are also different forms which exhibit life, consciousness, which is the symptom of the soul within. Therefore, a person in divine consciousness displays respect for and is friendly toward all living beings. He can see that they are all parts and parcels of God. This is how the devotee, who is equal to a topmost yogi, sees the Lord everywhere and is thus never lost to God. As Lord Krishna explains elsewhere:

"A true yogi observes Me in all beings, and also sees every being in Me. Indeed, the self-realized man sees Me everywhere. For one who sees Me everywhere and sees everything in Me, I am never lost, nor is he ever lost to Me. The yogi who knows that I and the Supersoul within all creatures are one worships Me and remains always in Me in all circumstances." (Bg.6.29-31)

DAY SIXTEEN: THERE IS LIFE AFTER DEATH

"As the embodied soul continually passes in this body from boyhood to youth to old age, the soul similarly passes into another body at death. The self-realized soul is not bewildered by such a change." (Bg.2.13)

"As a person puts on new garments, giving up old ones, similarly the soul accepts new material bodies, giving up the old and useless ones." (Bg.2.22)

* * *

As we can see, our body changes as we grow. It produces new cells, changes shape, we get taller, and then after middle age when we have stopped growing upward we often start growing outward. We first have a baby's body, then a child's, then a young person's body, and later an old body. So the body may be healthy, fit and athletic while young, but sickly, wrinkled and slow while old. However, the person inside the old body may still have the same desires or ambitions of a youth, but no longer has a body that can do the things he wants to do. So we are witnesses of the changes that the body goes through. This means we are inside yet different from the body we inhabit. Similarly, as our body changes in this life, we change bodies at the time of death. Yet, if we realize our difference from the material vehicle, we can be free of bewilderment or distress when we are forced to give up the present form. This is compared to changing clothes. Naturally, if we are eternal, as previously established, our existence does not stop with the death of the body. It goes on. If we are aware of our spiritual identity at the time of death, then such a change will not bewilder us.

However, what we do in this life will determine what kind of body we will get in the next. The Earth planet is like a portal that allows us to enter into any of the other dimensions that exist. By our actions and thoughts, which are forms of meditation, we develop a particular type of consciousness. That consciousness at the time of death will take us to the form of existence that is most suitable for us. And one thing that has a strong impression on shaping our consciousness is the type of worship we do. That is why Lord Krishna explains the best thing we should do:

"Those who worship the demigods will take birth among the demigods; those who worship ghosts and spirits will take birth among such beings; those who worship ancestors go to the ancestors; and those who worship Me will live with Me." (Bg.9.25)

DAY SEVENTEEN: GETTING THE HIGHER TASTE OF SPIRITUAL LIFE

"The embodied soul may be restricted from sense enjoyment, though the taste for it remains. But ceasing such engagement by experiencing a higher taste, he is fixed in consciousness." (Bg.2.59)

* * *

It is not enough to merely repress our sensual desires or urges. You may be able to do that for some time, but at some point they may come out in some other form, possibly as anger, violence, or basic discontent or frustration. This is also unhealthy as is trying to satisfy all of your desires, which is not so easy either, as previously explained.

After you begin to realize your eternal nature and become increasingly free from bodily desires, the only way you can completely rise above the urges of the senses is by connecting with the spiritual strata and experiencing the higher taste of transcendental bliss.

Such bliss, which is intrinsic to the soul, is awakened when one revives the soul's original status as a servant of God. This bliss is tasted in the mood of servitude, which is the natural, constitutional position of the soul.

In the material world we are always serving

something. It may be our spouse, children, employer, the government, or our mind and senses. We may not even want to serve, but are forced to do so. We are naturally engaged in serving. Of course, when we serve those we love, there is happiness in that. But the deeper happiness of the soul is reached when we dovetail our serving propensity and need to love toward the Supreme Being. He is the Supreme Lover, and the ultimate reciprocation and bliss can be attained when we direct our need to serve and love toward God. That is when we experience the higher taste from the spiritual platform that far outweighs the pleasure we get from sense enjoyment. For those who have reached this higher bliss, serving the senses will appear like a waste of time.

So as one increasingly experiences spiritual happiness, such a person's concern for pleasant surroundings and facilities will also decrease. This does not mean that the person will simply stop caring about his living conditions, but he becomes more detached and has less regard for such things. He is naturally happier with whatever comes along. He is more easily content with simpler arrangements and is happier with the freedom for pursuing spiritual life. However, as one experiences this, such a person will understand the real value of it and will also want to share this and give to others the means for attaining spiritual bliss of their own. As more people get connected to this higher taste, it can indeed spread to change the whole world. That is certainly something worth working for.

DAY EIGHTEEN: GOD REWARDS YOU ACCORDING TO YOUR DEEDS

"All of them–as they surrender unto Me–I reward accordingly. Everyone follows My path in all respects, O son of Pritha." (Bg.4.11)

* * *

As previously pointed out, we are rewarded with certain results according to what we do in life. And according to our level of surrender and approach to God, He reveals Himself to us.

Naturally, everything we see is a display of God's energies. Thus, no matter whether it is rocks or gold, ghosts or demigods, the effulgent Brahman or Krishna himself, we are all interacting with different levels of Krishna's energy. And we will get the degree of reciprocation that is available on that level. But when we focus our attention directly on Krishna, He rewards us according to the degree of our approach to Him and the love we have developed.

In this way, the purer and more intent we become, the more He rewards us with higher levels of insight and revelation of our relationship with Him. And those people who want to stay far away certainly are given the free will to remain far away from Krishna, at least in appearances and in their way of thinking. Otherwise, Lord Krishna is never far away from anyone or anything. Out of His causeless mercy He remains next to everyone and is the basis of everything as the Supersoul, Paramatma, in everyone's heart. Thus, Krishna rewards everyone equally, according to the degree of their desire to be with Him and understand Him.

DAY NINETEEN: OFFERING SERVICE TO GOD BRINGS FREEDOM

"Work done as an offering to Vishnu has to be performed, otherwise work binds one to this material world. Therefore, perform your prescribed duties for His satisfaction, and in that way you will always remain unattached and free from bondage." (Bg.3.9)

"One who works in devotion, who is a pure soul, and who controls his mind and senses, is dear to everyone, and everyone is dear to him. Though always working, such a man is never entangled." (Bg.5.7)

"The steadily devoted soul attains unadulterated peace because he offers the result of all activities to Me; whereas a person who is not in union with the Divine, who is greedy for the fruits of his labor, becomes entangled." (Bg.5.12)

* * *

Here in these verses we see how a person gets the results of his or her actions. Work done selfishly, for one's own pleasure or development, without considering its effects on others or the consequences, will certainly bind one to this material world. This describes the process of accumulating karma, which must be worked out through as many lifetimes as is necessary to arrive at a complete balance of all one's actions. Practically speaking, however, to arrive at such a balance is impossible without incorporating the spiritual path into our life. All activities will have some degree of fault in them, which will entail karma and future births, which may be pleasant or miserable, heavenly or hellish.

So the only way we can become free from this karmic cycle of repeated births and deaths is to learn how to begin engaging in the service of the Lord. This consists of the genuine spiritual activities that nullify all of our karma, both good and bad. That is the way to be unentangled or get free from being bound to the ups and downs of material existence. Offering our service or the results of our activities to the Lord is the path to freedom.

DAY TWENTY: HOW TO SERVE GOD

"O son of Kunti [Arjuna], all that you do, all that you eat, all that you offer and give away, as well as all austerities that you may perform, should be done as an offering to Me." (Bg.9.27)

"Engage your mind always in thinking of Me, offer obeisances and worship Me. Being completely absorbed in Me, surely you will come to Me." (Bg.9.34)

"Acts of sacrifice, charity and penance are not to be given up but should be performed. Indeed, sacrifice, charity and penance purify even the great souls." (Bg.18.5)

"In all activities just depend upon Me and work always under My protection. In such devotional service, be fully conscious of Me. If you become conscious of Me, you will pass over all the obstacles of conditional life by My grace." (Bg.18.57-58)

"Of vibrations I am the transcendental om. Of sacrifices I am the chanting of the holy names [japa]." (Bg.10.25)

"This divine energy of Mine, consisting of the three modes of material nature, is difficult to overcome. But those who have surrendered unto Me can easily cross beyond it." (Bg.7.14)

"Because you are My very dear friend, I am speaking to you the most confidential part of knowledge. Hear this from Me, for it is for your benefit. Always think of Me and become My devotee. Worship Me and offer your homage unto Me. Thus you will come to Me without fail. I promise you this because you are My very dear friend. Abandon all varieties of religion and just surrender unto Me. I shall deliver you from all sinful reactions. Do not fear." (Bg.18.64-66)

* * *

The above verses provide the formula for how best to serve God in a way that God most appreciates. It is said that you should not try to see God but act in such a way that God will see you. Then He will reveal Himself to you. So how do you act in that way? These verses make it easy to understand how to set aside some time each day to devote yourself to God. This is especially effective in the early morning. That is the most peaceful time of the day, the most powerful, and when the mind is the most receptive. At that time, whatever you do is most likely to carry the positive impressions with you throughout the day. Just taking some time for reflection, meditation and worship toward the Supreme is itself an act of sacrifice for spiritual progress.

So, this is how we learn to dedicate as much as we can as an offering to God, whether it is all we do, all we eat, all austerities or hardships we perform to become spiritualized. The point is to do it as a means of pleasing God. Even our job and the time we spend working becomes spiritualized when we do it as a means of offering the results for the devotional service to Lord Krishna.

You can go to the temple to do your worship, or stay at home and study the scripture, meditate, or also chant the holy names [japa]. As is mentioned in these verses, Krishna is the sacrifice of chanting His holy names. This means He appears within the sound vibration of His holy names, which can be perceived by one who properly chants them. The best mantra for doing this is the Hare Krishna mantra, which is Hare Krishna, Hare Krishna, Krishna Krishna, Hare Hare / Hare Rama, Hare Rama, Rama Rama, Hare Hare.

The main thing is to engage the mind in thinking of God. In this way, things like acts of sacrificing your time or giving charity to your local temple can be done as an offering to the Lord which spiritually purifies a person. Then throughout the day, depend on God and be conscious of Him as much as practically possible.

It is said that by remembering God even hell can be like heaven, and by forgetting God even heaven can become like hell. So by being always conscious of God, we can pass over so many obstacles. Knowing how to become conscious of God is the most confidential part of spiritual knowledge. And the essence of that is to always think of God by some means or other and never forget Him, as well as worship Him and offer your activities to Him, as He explains in the above verses. If we take this and give up all other forms of religion and simply concentrate on this process of thinking of the Lord, and in this way surrender to Him, we will certainly come to Him. This is His promise to us. Thus, there is no reason to fear. If we follow this process, we will be delivered.

DAY TWENTY-ONE: DEVOTIONAL SERVICE TO GOD BRINGS MOKSHA–LIBERATION

"A person who accepts the path of devotional service is not bereft of the results derived from studying the Vedas, performing austere sacrifices, giving charity or pursuing philosophical and fruitive activities. At the end he reaches the supreme abode." (Bg.8.28)

"My dear Arjuna, one who is engaged in My pure devotional service, free from the contamination of previous activities and from mental speculation, who is friendly to every living entity, certainly comes to Me." (Bg.11.55)

"Though engaged in all kinds of activities, My devotee, under My protection, reaches the eternal and imperishable abode by My grace." (Bg.18.56)

"That abode of Mine is not illumined by the sun or moon, nor by electricity. One who reaches it never returns to this material world." (Bg.15.6)

* * *

Again we need to realize the special nature of devotional service to Lord Krishna. It is the epitome of spiritual understanding. This is Vedanta, the end of all Vedic study. By reaching this conclusion, the results of all other processes are included, whether it be studying the Vedas, doing intense austerities, giving charity to altruistic purposes, or attaining whatever else that is offered by any other religion. It is indeed the culmination of all religious practice and inquiry. It is that which all other philosophical research and religious pursuits eventually lead. But you are being given it now.

Devotional service is the process of using the material body and engaging it in the direct service of the Lord. It purifies us of all karma and activities. It is the means of engaging in the same devotional service that goes on by those already liberated and serving God in the spiritual world. Thus, by following this system we will certainly attain the Supreme abode of the Lord, and, thus, never return to the material worlds. There is no goal or purpose higher than this.

DAY TWENTY-TWO: WHAT IF I CANNOT DO IT RIGHT?

"Just fix your mind upon Me, the Supreme Personality of Godhead, and engage all your intelligence in Me. Thus you will live in Me always, without a doubt. My dear Arjuna, if you cannot fix your mind upon Me without deviation, then follow the regulated principles of bhakti-yoga. In this way you will develop a desire to attain to Me. If you cannot practice the regulations of bhakti-yoga, then just try to work for Me, because by working for Me you will come to the perfect stage. If, however, you are unable to work in this consciousness, then try to act giving up all results of your work and try to be self-situated. If you cannot take to this practice, then engage yourself in the cultivation of knowledge. Better than knowledge, however, is meditation, and better than meditation is renunciation of the fruits of action, for by such renunciation one can attain peace of mind." (Bg.12.8-12)

* * *

At times we may have doubts that we will be successful on the spiritual path, or we may feel that we may not be able to continue because of various reasons or obstacles. Or maybe we think our mind simply gives us too much trouble.

Do not be troubled. Here in these verses Lord

Krishna gives the solutions. The best way is to fix the mind and intelligence on Him by any means available. But if that cannot be done at times, then there are other recommended things you can do to help control the mind, or stay focused and work toward the essential goal. So simply take up whatever level is best for you, as described above. Then work up the ladder of spiritual success of always remembering God. There is no pressure, and, as previously explained, whatever progress you make is eternal and helps to keep you moving forward.

    Here Lord Krishna simply explains that the best position is to fix the mind and intelligence in various ways on Him. If you cannot do that so easily, then observe the principles of bhakti-yoga since the process will help you increase your thoughts and affection towards God. If that cannot be done, then dedicating one's work and activities to God will also help. If you cannot adopt that attitude, then you can also offer the results of your work to God and remain free from greed. Or you can learn spiritual knowledge about the position of God, His activities and personality, along with the nature of your own spiritual identity. Or you can simply meditate on the Deity form of the Lord and the descriptions of His pastimes, or even give up the fruits or results of your actions. This can be done by doing service in the temple or to your Deity of God, and so on. Of course, a person can do all of these at different times, since they all assist in our spiritual development and the attainment of God consciousness. Thus, the Vedic path of spiritual progress is most flexible and broad in scope, and allows someone to approach God from any position in life.

    There may also be some people who may not have any inclination for spiritual practice. For them, it just does not grab their interest. Nonetheless, they may simply hear about the Lord from others and still worship the Supreme Being as best they can. Because they merely accept advice and instructions from spiritual authorities and observe the worship of the Lord, either at home or in the temples, they can also reach success on this path of devotional service. As Lord Krishna explains:

"There are those who, although not conversant in spiritual knowledge, begin to worship the Supreme Person upon hearing about Him from others. Because of their tendency to hear from authorities, they also transcend the path of birth and death." (Bg.13.26)

So, decide which of these you wish to do and make them a regular part of your spiritual practice.

DAY TWENTY-THREE: EVEN IF YOU MAKE A MISTAKE, YOU ARE SAVED

"Even if you are considered to be the most sinful of all sinners, when you are situated in the boat of transcendental knowledge, you will be able to cross over the ocean of miseries." (Bg.4.36)

"Even if one commits the most abominable actions, if he is engaged in devotional service, he is to be considered saintly because he is properly situated. He or she quickly becomes righteous and attains lasting peace. O son of Kunti [Arjuna], declare it boldly that My devotee never perishes." (Bg.9.30-31)

* * *

All right, so what if you make a mistake along the way? Or what if you made so many mistakes or sinful activities before accepting this path? Some people may wonder if they have a chance? But do not let things like this make you depressed, upset or ready to give up. I have already explained that whatever you can do gives eternal benefit. So feeling like quitting is just another temporary mood of an unfriendly mind. We have to control this and stay focused on the goal, which is attained over the long-term with faithful and steady progress. However, it can also be attained immediately, depending on how sincere we are.

As Lord Krishna says here, even if we have been the worst of sinners, if we accept this path and enter the boat of spiritual knowledge and follow it sincerely, we become purified of our previous acts and can cross this ocean of material existence to the spiritual domain.

Even if one is on this path yet for some reason makes some mistakes, if he or she is apologetic for them and continues to seriously engage in devotional service, then one will still be rightly situated. He will again become purified of such mistakes. Of course, this does not mean that you make a plan to engage in questionable activities while thinking you will again become freed from the reactions of them by your devotional service. That will not work. You will still be held accountable. In fact, to think that you can engage in sinful activities and then be free from the reactions by the performance of devotional service is offensive. And too much of such nonsense spoils your spiritual service. But those who are serious and enthusiastic about spiritual life and try their best, despite some mistakes along the way, can take courage because Lord Krishna explains that His devotee never perishes. He is always protected, and at the time of death he or she can reach the spiritual abode.

DAY TWENTY-FOUR: UNDERSTANDING THE DIVINE NATURE OF GOD

"Whenever and wherever there is a decline in religious practice, and a predominant rise of irreligion–at that time I descend Myself. In order to deliver the pious and to annihilate the miscreants, as well as to reestablish the principles of religion, I advent Myself millennium after millennium. One who knows this transcendental nature of My appearance and activities does not, upon leaving the body, take his birth again in this material world, but attains My eternal abode." (Bg.4.7-9)

"I am the source of all spiritual and material worlds. Everything emanates from Me. The wise who know this perfectly engage in My devotional service and worship Me with all their hearts." (Bg.10.8)

* * *

These verses describe the importance of understanding the divine nature of God. God is always the source of all spiritual and material worlds and, therefore, never comes under control of His own creation. Thus, He can enter and exit it at will. And He does so to protect dharma and the spiritual path for the benefit of the masses. However, if He has His representatives or pure devotees present to protect and preserve His instructions and the path of dharma, then that is just as good as His personal presence. Society can still take advantage of it, which is essential.

This is why Lord Krishna comes to deliver the pious. But He also comes to annihilate the miscreants. So this also means that there may be times when drastic measures must be taken to protect the dharma if it is threatened by others who want to damage or alter it, or make it extinct. So Krishna's representatives must also be able to stand up for what is right and do what is necessary if there are those who want to destroy the dharma.

As Sri Krishna explains, by understanding His divine nature and the reasons for His appearance in this world, we do not take birth in this material creation again. Such wise persons, knowing that the Lord is the origination of everything, certainly engage in the devotional service to the Lord with all their hearts.

DAY TWENTY-FIVE: UNDERSTANDING THE POWER OF THE LORD

"Of all that is material and all that is spiritual in this world, know for certain that I am both its origin and dissolution. There is no Truth superior to Me. Everything rests upon Me as pearls are strung on a thread." (Bg.7.6-7)

"Those who know Me as the Supreme Lord, as the governing principle of the material manifestation, who know Me as the one underlying all the demigods and as the one sustaining all sacrifices, can, with steadfast mind, understand and know Me even at the time of death." (Bg7.30)

"Those who are not deluded, the great souls, are under the protection of the divine nature. They are fully engaged in devotional service because they know Me as the Supreme Personality of Godhead, original and inexhaustible." (Bg.9.13)

"I am the father of this universe, the mother, the support, and the grandsire. I am the object of knowledge, the purifier and the syllable om. I am also the Rig, the Sama and the Yajur [Vedas]. I am the goal, the sustainer, the master, the witness, the abode, the refuge and the most dear friend. I am the creation and the annihilation, the basis of everything, the resting place and the eternal seed." (Bg.9.17-18)

"One can understand the Supreme Personality as He is only by devotional service. And when one is in full consciousness of the Supreme Lord by such devotion, he can enter into the kingdom of God." (Bg.18.55)

* * *

These verses will help us to further understand the power and position of the Supreme Being. Read them and meditate on them. It is only through the devotional attitude by which one can understand God, and is the cause of reciprocation between the Lord and His devotee. This love is what brings the Lord to reveal Himself to His devotee. And even those of us who may not be completely pure but are sincere can still get a glimpse of this exchange and how the Lord reveals Himself to us. Remember, sincerity is the essence of purity. With that, God can give you whatever else you need.

The point is to understand and focus your mind on God, especially at the time of death. By doing that, it is certain one will enter the kingdom of God, and leave this material world hundreds of times faster than a rocket traveling through the sky. Even now, as a devotee, when sitting quietly thinking of God, we should feel ourselves zooming out of this material world. Understanding the knowledge in these verses is all that it takes. So read them again. As we absorb this information and engage in devotion to God, we come under the influence and protection of the divine nature. This helps move us forward in our comprehension of our eternal relationship with God. As we absorb our consciousness in devotion toward the Lord, we can certainly enter into the kingdom of God.

DAY TWENTY-SIX: STAYING CLOSE TO GOD

"And of all yogis, he who abides in Me with great faith, worshiping Me in transcendental loving service, is most intimately united with Me in yoga and is the highest of all." (Bg.6.47)

"To those who are constantly devoted and worship Me with love, I give the understanding by which they can come to Me. Out of compassion for them, I, dwelling in their hearts, destroy with the shining lamp of knowledge the darkness born of ignorance." (Bg.10.10-11)

"The Blessed Lord said: He whose mind is fixed on My personal form, always engaged in worshiping Me with great and transcendental faith, is considered by Me to be most perfect." (Bg.12.2)

"One who is not envious but who is a kind friend to all living entities, who does not think himself a proprietor, who is free from false ego and equal both in happiness and distress, who is always satisfied and engaged in devotional service with determination and whose mind and intelligence are in agreement with Me–he is very dear to Me." (Bg.12.13-14)

"One who is equal to friends and enemies, who is equipoised in honor and dishonor, heat and cold, happiness and distress, fame and infamy, who is always free from contamination, always silent and satisfied with anything, who doesn't care for any residence, who is fixed in knowledge and engaged in devotional service, is very dear to Me." (Bg.12.18-19)

* * *

In these verses we learn the qualities and characteristics and even some of the behavior of a person who is dear to the Lord. We can go over these verses repeatedly to remind ourselves of what we need to attain that position. It is actually not so difficult. It is simply a matter of incorporating the previous points that have been outlined in this course. Then, as instructed above, we focus on abiding in the Lord with great faith, worshiping Him in transcendental loving service, being devoted to Him in love, and concentrating on His personal form as Lord Krishna.

We are always very dear to the Lord, but especially when we see all situations and all living beings equally with spiritual vision and are engaged in His service as much as our time allows. The more we can remember the Lord, the more He reciprocates and give us additional insights of knowledge that destroys the darkness of ignorance which holds us back from progressing spiritually. Thus, we approach ever closer to Him. And the more we try to get close to God, the closer He gets to us. So with God's help and our sincere desire, we remain close to Him.

DAY TWENTY-SEVEN: TOLERATING THOSE WHO DON'T CARE FOR GOD

"Those miscreants who are grossly foolish, lowest among mankind, whose knowledge is stolen by illusion, or who partake of the atheistic nature of demons, do not surrender unto Me." (Bg.7.15)

"I am never manifest to the foolish and unintelligent. For them I am covered by My eternal creative potency [yoga-maya]; and so the deluded world knows Me not, who am unborn and infallible." (Bg.7.25)

"Fools deride Me when I descend in the human form. They do not know My transcendental nature and My supreme dominion over all that be." (Bg.9.11)

"Arrogance, pride, anger, conceit, harshness and ignorance–these qualities belong to those of demonic nature, O son of Pritha" (Bg.16.4)

* * *

Naturally, while living in this material world we will come in contact with those who are not inclined toward religious or spiritual practice. Maybe they believe in God but just are not so interested. This can be tolerated. And generally they may not ridicule religious practice. So, some of these people may still be engaged in small amounts of service to God or discussions about God, but not much else should be expected from them. However, I have seen a few of such people change and later become strong devotees. But you have to approach them very carefully.

Others, however, may be outright atheists who want nothing to do with anything that deals with God. You might say that atheists are merely those who have no faith because they are spiritually inexperienced. They are like children that have little or no background but may say anything without proper education or investigation. Of course, this is the material creation where everyone has the freedom to believe what they like. But in the above verses it is described that their lack of faith is due to foolishness, illusion, or because of sinful or demonic activities and attitudes. Those who are covered by darkness due to wicked motivations never surrender to the Lord or engage in devotional service. If they appear to do so, it is for ulterior motives and desires. But such people are especially demonic if they deride religion or God, or are harsh and insulting to those engaged in the service of God. Such people will never understand the Supreme Being, nor will God reveal Himself to them, except in the form of the final lesson of death. Then they will be forced to submit to the power of God that causes their body to shut down and kicks them into a different situation.

In any case, such a person should be avoided. It is not that we want to try to engage him in discussions about spiritual topics or try to persuade them toward accepting spiritual reality. It may only make them disturbed and give them more opportunity to make offenses to us and to God. We do not need to try to make their karma any worse than it is. And we do not give our reasons and purpose over to the contradiction of foolish men. So we merely remain polite to such persons, wish them well, smile and keep walking.

However, if we are bold enough, we may prepare some nice food, sweets or something anyone will like, offer it to the Deity or picture of God which then makes it *prasada*, sacred food. Then we can offer some of it to our atheistic or demonic acquaintances. Of course, we do not tell them it is *prasada*. We just offer it as a friend. In any way that people may come in contact with spiritual substance, it has its affect. Like fire, whether you understand it or not, it will burn if you touch it. Similarly, genuine spirituality in any form always produces positive results.

DAY TWENTY-EIGHT: YOUR SPECIAL POSITION AS GOD'S DEVOTEE

"After many births and deaths, he who is actually in knowledge surrenders unto Me, knowing Me to be the cause of all causes and all that is. Such a great soul is very rare." (Bg.7.19)

"Four kinds of pious men render devotional service

unto Me–the distressed, the desirer of wealth, the inquisitive, and he who is searching for knowledge of the Absolute... All these devotees are undoubtedly magnanimous souls, but he who is situated in knowledge of Me I consider verily to dwell in Me. Being engaged in My transcendental service, he attains Me." (Bg.7.16, 18)

"Intelligent persons who are endeavoring for liberation from old age and death take refuge in Me in devotional service." (Bg.7.29)

"Always chanting My glories, endeavoring with great determination, bowing down before Me, these great souls perpetually worship Me with devotion." (Bg.9.14)

"I envy no one, nor am I partial to anyone. I am equal to all. But whoever renders service unto Me in devotion is a friend, is in Me, and I am also a friend to him." (Bg.9.29)

"He who follows this imperishable path of devotional service and who completely engages himself with faith, making Me the supreme goal, is very, very dear to Me." (Bg.12.20)

* * *

Now we can see how special is the position of being a devotee of the Lord. It is very rare to attain. One gets the opportunity to be a devotee in only two ways: 1) You have to qualify yourself after many lifetimes of pursuing the spiritual path, or 2) you receive and intelligently accept the mercy of another pure devotee, which itself is the merciful arrangement of God.

The people who become devotees of God, engaged in His devotional service in various ways, are described here by Lord Krishna as great souls, a friend to Him, and very, very dear to Him. So when a person is regarded by God in such a way, their position is secure. In this situation all we have to do is keep following the spiritual path of devotion and entrance into the spiritual domain after death is guaranteed. However, on this platform we only pray to be an instrument of God, to do the will of God, and be channels through which comes peace and spiritual knowledge. So, if He calls us to go back home to the spiritual worlds, that will be the greatest day of our lives. Yet, if He wants us to stay in this material creation to do something else, then we readily accept that as well. If our consciousness is spiritualized, then it does not matter where we are, because we see God everywhere and we remain close to Him. Our very being is spiritually surcharged. Thus, in any situation, we are already home. We are already in the spiritual domain because that is what we perceive when our consciousness is saturated with transcendental frequency.

DAY TWENTY-NINE: BE GREAT BY BEING AN EXAMPLE FOR OTHERS

"Whatever action is performed by a great man, common men follow in his footsteps. And whatever standards he sets by exemplary acts, all the world pursues." (Bg.3.21)

* * *

If being a devotee is a rare position as previously established, then we should not feel proud. We surrender to God to humble ourselves to reach a higher point, a higher and clearer connection to God. This does not mean that we become so humble that we are the doormat for everyone else, or get easily pushed around. But we free ourselves from the complex details of life by knowing that if we do God's will, and connect with His intent, then that energy can flow through us to reach others. To be a good servant of God we must also be a reflection of God's unconditional love for us. We must be a vehicle through which God's love can come through to reach everyone else. We see everyone else as part of God's family. That is true greatness.

We are all born sensitive, but the details of life

often desensitize us. We cannot allow life to do that to us. We have to remain aware of others' feelings, pain, and needs and be able to respond to that in a humane and spiritual way. We have to remember that the more we help or assist others, the more we also help ourselves. We have to do that because we are the ones who need the help. This attitude will keep us humble as well as focused on what is our real purpose, and empowered to keep in mind our own spiritual position as the devotee of God. We have to remember that if we love God, we will also love all of His energy and His innumerable parts and parcels.

So, we need to see the example of what should be done. We may become great teachers or not. Being great and being popular are two different things. And being popular without being truly great can be very dangerous. That has brought about the end of many people. If you are popular but not great, then when you fall, everyone will be watching everything that happens to you. So we need to be great in the essential spiritual standards, no matter whether anyone else notices or not. We have to set the example. That itself is often the best way to teach. As these standards are presented, others will follow and accept the example you have set. Or they will at least respect it.

There is an old saying that the world never knows its greatest men. It is better to be like that than to think you are great and infallible, and then become popular only to later fall down from your position and cause others to become disturbed by having their faith crushed.

So be a great devotee by being humble yet strong, being kind and merciful yet firm, and by being loving but fair and equal. And most of all, be an instrument and representative of God that all can view with respect and admiration.

DAY THIRTY: BEING DELIVERED AT THE TIME OF DEATH

"He who meditates on the Supreme Personality of Godhead, his mind constantly engaged in remembering Me, undeviated from the path, he, O Partha [Arjuna], is sure to reach Me." (Bg.8.8)

"For one who remembers Me without deviation, I am easy to obtain, O son of Pritha [Arjuna], because of his constant engagement in devotional service. After attaining Me, the great souls, who are yogis in devotion, never return to this temporary world, which is full of miseries, because they have attained the highest perfection. From the highest planet in the material world down to the lowest, all are places of misery wherein repeated birth and death take place. But one who attains to My abode never takes birth again." (Bg.8.14-16)

"Whatever state of being one remembers when he quits his body, that state will be attained without fail." (Bg.8.6) "And whoever, at the time of death, quits his body remembering Me alone, at once attains My nature. Of this there is no doubt." (Bg.8.5)

* * *

Lord Krishna says here that all of the planets in this material world are places of misery. This is not our real home nor where we are meant to be. It is all temporary wherein we undergo the continual drama of repeated birth and death. How many times is enough? So we should not be overly attached to anything in this creation when we leave this body.

So, as we pursue this spiritual path and make progress, it becomes increasingly easier to think of God. And those that do will certainly find it easy to think of God at the time of their death. The only reason why people cannot think of the Supreme when they are leaving the body is because they do not practice during life. This is the purpose of the spiritual path, to give you that practice.

Otherwise, people may occupy themselves with a million other things but leave out what is most important. Thus, at the time of death their consciousness dwells on those other things. In fact, in any yoga system or religion, this is the ultimate goal–to be able to think or meditate on God at the moment one leaves the body. This allows one to return to God and leave this material existence behind.

As stated in the above verses, whatever our state of consciousness is at the time of death, we take that with us into our next life. In fact, what we are thinking of when we leave this body directs us toward our next existence. So it is very important to attain the right level of consciousness by the time we die, and to easily be thinking of the right thoughts and objects at the moment of death. Those who think of Lord Krishna at that time certainly attain His nature and reach His spiritual abode. Once one has attained the spiritual planets, birth in the material worlds never takes place again.

DAY THIRTY-ONE: SHARING THIS MESSAGE

"For one who explains this supreme secret to the devotees, devotional service is guaranteed, and at the end he will come back to Me. There is no servant in this world more dear to Me than he, nor will there ever be one more dear. And I declare that he who studies this sacred conversation worships Me by his intelligence. And one who listens with faith and without envy becomes free from sinful reaction and attains to the planets where the pious dwell." (Bg.18.68-71)

* * *

Here we can understand how powerful are the words and instructions of Lord Krishna. Simply reading the *Bhagavad-gita*, the conversation between Lord Krishna and Arjuna, is a form of worship and meditation that utilizes one's intelligence. This itself is part of the process of purifying our consciousness. Merely listening with faith cleanses one of the reactions to numerous sinful activities and allows that person to enter the heavenly planets of the pious. Therefore, reading *Bhagavad-gita* on a regular basis should be done. Setting up functions for the benefit of the general mass of people for reading and explaining *Bhagavad-gita* should also be encouraged. It will certainly spread a positive energy and spiritually charge the atmosphere in the community, especially for all who participate.

Lord Krishna also explains that those who spread and explain this message to others will certainly attain devotional service. Actually, such activity is direct service to God by spreading His message. And Krishna also says that there is no servant of His who is more dear than one who engages in this service. Some servants take great risks going all over the world to deliver this message to the people in general. So we can only imagine how much affection Krishna has for them. By looking at the world's present condition and all the crime, war and quarrel that is going on, we can understand the need in society to be uplifted and to rise to a higher level of cooperation and peace, then we can also agree that the whole world would be greatly benefitted by hearing the Lord's instructions. Therefore, we should make a point to share this spiritual knowledge with those around us. As we provide the means for the success of others, our own success is also guaranteed.

CONCLUSION

By following these points that are presented from the *Bhagavad-gita*, you can see how easy it is to practice this essence of the Vedic path and be assured of success. You only need to be serious, faithful, and sincere. Associate with other like-minded people and devotees, and add the principles outlined herein to your lives. You will quickly begin to see a difference in your life, your attitude, your interactions with others, and in your own relationship with God. I also wish you all success.

CHAPTER FOUR

Bhagavad-gita's Ultimate Purpose

The *Bhagavad-gita* is the essence of all Vedic philosophy and is composed of 700 verses and explains such topics as the nature of the soul, God, the material universe, the nature of activities and karma, reincarnation, the process of yoga, the purpose of life, and more. Within the *Bhagavad-gita* we can find the teachings for such additional topics as how to have a peaceful life, how to gain stability of mind, how to understand the workings of material nature, or even get insights into principles of management. When we really analyze it, there are so many different levels of understanding that can be found within it. Nonetheless, in the *Bhagavad-gita* we find a recurring theme which puts emphasis on what Lord Krishna taught and expected of Arjuna, and all readers of it, for what we really need to accomplish, and the real purpose of it. Out of all of the teachings we find within, Bhagavan Sri Krishna continues to emphasize the need to end our karma, to stop the cycle of birth and death in this material existence, and to ultimately reach the spiritual world, His abode, where we belong.

These verses form what can be called part of the foundation of the bhakti movement in emphasizing devotion to Krishna as the Supreme Being, which also provides the means to free ourselves from *samsara*, repeated birth and death in this material creation, and attain the highest spiritual destination. This would also place attention on Kurukshetra, the Dharma-dhama, also called

Dharmakshetra, since this is the place where Lord Krishna taught this most crucial of information, as found in the *Bhagavad-gita*. Therefore, the land of Kurukshetra should be considered one of the most important places for not only the bhakti movement, but also as the historical place of origination for these most essential teachings on Vedic Dharma, and where these teachings were most effectively put into action with the battle of Kurukshetra. What follows are a number of the verses which explain this most essential recurring theme as emphasized by Lord Sri Krishna.

Starting in Chapter 2, Content of the Gita Summarized, after Bhagavan Sri Krishna begins to teach the essential aspects of understanding the soul, He says in verse 72 the real purpose of this knowledge, which is how to follow this path to lead a life that will bring a person to the highest destination possible, "That is the way of the spiritual and godly life, after attaining which a man is not bewildered. Being so situated, even at the hour of death, one can enter into the kingdom of God." This is the beginning of recognizing that Lord Krishna wants Arjuna and all of us to ultimately attain the spiritual realm. This is the real purpose of His teachings in *Bhagavad-gita*.

Then in Chapter 4, Sri Krishna continues to clarify this in the explanations of what is Transcendental Knowledge and how to begin to comprehend Krishna as the Absolute Truth. In verse 9 He says, "One who knows the transcendental nature of My appearance and activities does not, upon leaving the body, take his birth again in this material world, but attains My eternal abode, O Arjuna."

In this way, understanding the truth and characteristics of Bhagavan Sri Krishna is one method that can bring a person to the spiritual world. But attaining the spiritual world is the main point.

Then in verses 23-24 of the same chapter, Lord Krishna again emphasizes that, "The work of a man who is unattached to the modes of material nature, and who is fully situated in transcendental knowledge, merges entirely into transcendence. A person who is fully absorbed in Krishna consciousness is sure to attain the spiritual kingdom because of his full contribution to spiritual activities, in which the consummation is absolute and that which is offered is of the same spiritual nature."

In other words, by engaging in bhakti-yoga, or the devotional service to the Supreme Lord, Sri Krishna, such activities are on the spiritual platform, cutting one off from material activities and their reactions, and spiritualizes one's consciousness, which is the goal, for that is the process for perceiving and then entering the spiritual abode.

Then in verse 30 of the same chapter, Lord Krishna makes it even more clear by explaining that when a person attains an attraction to performing loving devotional activities to Him, that attraction overcomes any material desires and takes one to the spiritual realm. As He says, "All these performers who know the meaning of sacrifice become cleansed of sinful reaction [meaning freedom from karma], and, having tasted the nectar of the remnants of such sacrifice [meaning to attain the attraction to performing spiritual activities], they go to the supreme eternal abode."

In verse 32 we find that He elaborates by saying, "All these different types of sacrifice are approved by the Vedas, and all of them are born of different types of work [meaning physical, mental, or intellectual]. Knowing them as such [to bring you above the bodily platform], you will become liberated."

In Chapter 5, when Krishna explains the process of Karma-yoga–Action in Krishna Consciousness, verses 24-26, Krishna again explains the spiritual goal of all such activities, which is the purpose of Karma-yoga, "One whose happiness is within, who is active within, who rejoices within and is illumined within, is actually the perfect mystic. He is liberated in the Supreme, and ultimately he attains the Supreme. One who is beyond duality and doubt, whose mind is engaged within, who is always busy working for the welfare of all sentient beings, and who is free from all sins, achieves liberation in the Supreme. Those who are free from anger and all material desires, who are self-realized, self-disciplined and constantly endeavoring for perfection, are assured of liberation in the Supreme in the very near future."

Here again the purpose of focusing all of our actions on the transcendental nature of who we are, and the means to free ourselves from all karma, is to ultimately attain liberation or freedom from the continuation of any more material existence.

Then in Chapter 7, Knowledge of the Absolute, Bhagavan Sri Krishna explains His different energies and to which energy the individual soul belongs. However, in verse 18, Lord Krishna emphasizes the central purpose of being His devotee, and how to most favorably reach the supreme goal: "All these devotees are undoubtedly magnanimous souls, but he who is situated in knowledge of Me I consider verily to dwell in Me. Being engaged in My transcendental service, he attains Me."

To elaborate further, in Chapter 8, Attaining the Supreme, verses 5-8, Lord Krishna clearly expresses the purpose of meditation and the ultimate goal for which we should practice through all the phases of our life. "And whoever, at the time of death, quits his body, remembering Me alone, at once attains My nature. Of this there is no doubt. Whatever state of being one remembers when he quits his body, that state he will attain without fail. Therefore, Arjuna, you should always think of Me in the form of Krishna and at the same time carry out your prescribed duty of fighting. With your activities dedicated to Me and your mind and intelligence fixed on Me, you will attain Me without doubt. He who meditates on the Supreme Personality of Godhead, his mind constantly engaged in remembering Me, undeviated from the path, he, O Partha [Arjuna], is sure to reach Me."

Again Lord Krishna further explains in Chapter 8,

verses 13-14, the ultimate way to prepare for leaving this body so we can attain the highest destination after this life: "After being situated in this yoga practice and vibrating the sacred syllable om, the supreme combination of letters, if one thinks of the Supreme Personality of Godhead and quits his body, he will certainly reach the spiritual planets. For one who remembers Me without deviation, I am easy to obtain, O son of Partha, because of his constant engagement in devotional service [bhakti-yoga]."

Lord Krishna makes the ultimate purpose of all of His instructions in the *Bhagavad-gita* very clear by again, in Chapter 8, verse 21, explaining that He expects us to ultimately attain His spiritual abode: "That supreme abode is called unmanifested and infallible, and it is the supreme destination. When one goes there, he never comes back. That is My supreme abode."

Therefore, in Chapter 9, The Most Confidential Knowledge, verse 25, Lord Krishna relates the destination of those who meditate on other objects of worship, while the real goal is to reach the spiritual realm of Lord Krishna. "Those who worship the demigods will take birth among the demigods; those who worship ghosts and spirits will take birth among such beings; those who worship ancestors go to the ancestors; and those who worship Me will live with Me."

Then in the same chapter, verse 28, Lord Krishna points us in what He considers the right direction to attain the highest goal, when He says, "In this way you will be freed from all reactions to good and evil deeds, and by this principle of renunciation you will be liberated and come to Me."

However, Lord Krishna is not yet finished in emphasizing the ultimate purpose of these instructions of *Bhagavad-gita*. He reiterates in verse 34, "Engage your mind always in thinking of Me, offer obeisances and worship Me. Being completely absorbed in Me, surely you will come to Me."

In this way, He explains the real objective, as He again points out in Chapter 13, verse 24, when speaking about Nature, the Enjoyer, and Consciousness, "One who understands this philosophy concerning material nature, the living entity and the interaction of the modes of nature is sure to attain liberation. He will not take birth here again, regardless of his present position."

Later in verse 35 of the same chapter, Lord Krishna points out that by perceiving the difference between the body and the person who resides in the body, the soul, leads us to becoming free from bodily existence. He says, "One who knowingly sees this difference between the body and the owner of the body and can understand the process of liberation from this bondage, also attains to the supreme goal."

This is the process of becoming free from illusion, in which Arjuna was temporarily entrapped by his confusion about what he should do. So to provide the whole purpose for attaining freedom from illusion and such misconceptions, Lord Sri Krishna instructs in Chapter 15, The Yoga of the Supreme Person, in verses 5-6, "One who is free from illusion, false prestige, and false association, who understands the eternal, who is done with material lust and is freed from the duality of happiness and distress, and who knows how to surrender unto the Supreme Person, attains to that eternal kingdom. That abode of Mine is not illumined by the sun or moon, nor by electricity. One who reaches it never returns to this material world."

Finally, after explaining the whole *Bhagavad-gita* to Arjuna, Lord Krishna reaches the culmination of all such Upanishadic knowledge by summarizing the ultimate goal of any devotee, when He says in Chapter 18, Conclusion– The Perfection of Renunciation, verses 55-56: "One can understand the Supreme Personality as He is only by devotional service [bhakti-yoga]. And when one is in full consciousness of the Supreme Lord by such devotion, he can enter into the kingdom of God. Though engaged in all kinds of activities, My devotee, under My protection, reaches the eternal and imperishable abode by My grace."

Therefore, the ultimate position of any transcendentalist or yogi is to attain the grace of the Lord if we want to enter the spiritual world or kingdom of God. And to do this most effectively, Lord Krishna clearly says, again in Chapter 18, verses 65-66: "Always think of Me and become My devotee. Worship Me and offer your homage unto Me. Thus you will come to Me without fail. I promise you this because you are My very dear friend. Abandon all varieties of religion and just surrender unto Me. I shall deliver you from all sinful reaction. Do not fear."

Herein is the final conclusion of the purpose of all spiritual activities, without which, we have still not quite attained or understood the goal. And for those who help illuminate this, Lord Krishna says in Chapter 18, verses 68-69, that such a person can certainly attain the goal of the teachings of *Bhagavad-gita*, "For one who explains this supreme secret to the devotees, devotional service is guaranteed, and at the end he will come back to Me. There is no servant in this world more dear to Me than he, nor will there ever be one more dear." So, in other words, teaching this knowledge is itself devotional service or bhakti-yoga, which is the basis for spiritualizing our consciousness, and which is the method for entering the spiritual abode of Lord Krishna.

In addition to this, simply by studying the *Bhagavad-gita* will lead to great achievements on our path of spiritual progress, as Lord Krishna explains in Chapter 18, verses 70-71: "And I declare that he who studies this sacred conversation worships Me by his intelligence. And one who listens with faith and without envy becomes free from sinful reaction and attains to the planets where the pious dwell."

It can't get easier than that.

* * *

To conclude, all of these verses quoted above, and many others from the *Bhagavad-gita* indicate the ultimate purpose of its teachings, and, quite honestly, the ultimate purpose behind all of Vedic knowledge. We are not really a product of this material creation, nor is it our real home, nor will we ever be able to stay here forever. So Lord Krishna emphasizes the real goal of life within this recurring theme in the *Bhagavad-gita*, which is to reach freedom from any further existence in this material world and attain Bhagavan Sri Krishna's supreme spiritual abode. That is our ultimate destination where we can attain the real nature of the soul, which reveals our true identity, and where we can finally be truly happy and blissful.

REFERENCE

The Bhagavad-gita As it Is, translated by A. C. Bhaktivedanta Swami, Bhaktivedanta Book Trust, New York/Los Angeles, 1972.

CONCLUSION

Your Next Step

After reading this introduction to the *Bhagavad-gita*, we hope you will be inclined to get your own copy of the *Bhagavad-gita* and study it yourself. I have several editions myself and have gone through all of them, but I do recommend most highly the edition called *The Bhagavad-gita As It Is* by His Divine Grace A. C. Bhaktivedanta Swami Prabhupada. It is one of the most authorized editions which includes the Sanskrit for each verse, followed by the Roman transliteration of the verse, word for word translation, then the English verse itself, with a purport to help explain the meaning of the verse, along with beautiful pictures to help illustrate the philosophy. You can find this edition in many different online outlets.

Also, since the *Bhagavad-gita* was spoken 5000 years ago in the holy town of Kurukshetra, at the place called Jyotisar, I suggest everyone in India and visitors to India to go and see this place first hand. Kurukshetra is also called Dharmakshetra as the place of Dharma since Lord Krishna spoke the *Bhagavad-gita* there. You will find many historical sites to see in Kurukshetra, and it is only about a three-hour drive north of Delhi, also reached by rail. So it is easy to reach. Besides, they are fixing many of these places to make them more tourist friendly, so it will be a beautiful addition to any tours you take of India.

There are also many temples such as the newly built Iskcon Krishna temple that is on the road going from town to Jyotisar, along with museums, kunds or holy ponds, and other historical places that help mark events that took place many hundreds of years ago, besides being where the battle described in the classic text called the *Mahabharata* took place. Some people drive there to spend a day to see what is most significant and return to Delhi or Vrindavana by night. Others spend a few days to see everything. I always spend a few days there, sometimes to attend the *Bhagavad-gita* conference at the Kurukshetra University, but I always like to see the sites there. It is one of my favorite places.

In the meantime, if you would like to take a little video tour of Kurukshetra, here is a video I made during one of my recent visits there. You can see it by using this link: https://www.youtube.com/watch?v=CbHTGc6PM3w

Or you can go on youtube.com and simply search for Visiting Kurukshetra by Stephen Knapp.

We hope this has been of assistance to you in not only understanding the potential of the *Bhagavad-gita*, but also in helping you understand the spiritual purpose of life.

GLOSSARY

Acarya--the spiritual master who sets the proper standard by his own example.

Advaita--nondual, meaning that the Absolute Truth is one, and that there is no individuality between the Supreme Being and the individual souls which merge into oneness, the Brahman, when released from material existence. The philosophy taught by Sankaracharya.

Agnihotra--the Vedic sacrifice in which offerings were made to the fire, such as ghee, milk, sesame seeds, grains, etc. The demigod Agni would deliver the offerings to the demigods that are referred to in the ritual.

Ahankara--false ego, identification with matter.

Ahimsa--nonviolence.

Akarma--actions which cause no *karmic* reactions.

Ananda--spiritual bliss.

Ananta--unlimited.

Arati--the ceremony of worship when incense and ghee lamps are offered to the Deities.

Arca-vigraha--the worshipable Deity form of the Lord made of stone, wood, etc.

Aryan--a noble person, one who is on the Vedic path of spiritual advancement.

Asana--postures for meditation, or exercises for developing the body into a fit instrument for spiritual advancement.

Asat--that which is temporary.

Ashrama--one of the four orders of spiritual life, such as *brahmacari* (celibate student), *grihastha* (married householder), *vanaprastha* (retired stage), and *sannyasa* (renunciate); or the abode of a spiritual teacher or *sadhu*.

Ashvamedha--a Vedic ritual involving offerings to God made by brahmana priests.

Astanga-yoga--the eightfold path of mystic yoga.

Asura--one who is ungodly or a demon.
Atma--the self or soul. Sometimes means the body, mind, and senses.
Atman--usually referred to as the Supreme Self.
Avatara--an incarnation of the Lord who descends from the spiritual world.
Avidya--ignorance or nescience.
Aum--om or *pranava*
Bhajan--song of worship.
Bhakta--a devotee of the Lord who is engaged in *bhakti-yoga*.
Bhakti--love and devotion for God.
Bhakti-yoga--the path of offering pure devotional service to the Supreme.
Brahma--the demigod of creation who was born from Lord Vishnu, the first created living being and the engineer of the secondary stage of creation of the universe when all the living entities were manifested.
Brahmacari--a celibate student, usually five to twenty-five years of age, who is trained by the spiritual master. One of the four divisions or *ashramas* of spiritual life.
Brahmajyoti--the great white light or effulgence which emanates from the body of the Lord.
Brahmaloka--the highest planet or plane of existence in the universe; the planet where Lord Brahma lives.
Brahman--the spiritual energy; the all-pervading impersonal aspect of the Lord; or the Supreme Lord Himself.
Brahmana or brahmin--one of the four orders of society; the intellectual class of men who have been trained in the knowledge of the *Vedas* and initiated by a spiritual master.
Chaitanya Mahaprabhu--the most recent incarnation of the Lord who appeared in the 15th century in Bengal and who originally started the *sankirtana* movement, based on

congregational chanting of the holy names.

Chakra--a wheel, disk, or psychic energy center situated along the spinal column in the subtle body of the physical shell.

Chhandas--sacred hymns of the *Atharva-veda*.

Deity--the *arca-vigraha*, or worshipful form of the Divinity in the temple.

Deva–a demigod, or higher being.

Devas--demigods or heavenly beings from higher levels of material existence, or a godly person.

Dham--a holy place.

Dharma--the essential nature or duty of the living being.

Dualism--as related in this book, it refers to the Supreme as both an impersonal force (Brahman) as well as the Supreme Person.

Dwaita--dualism, the principle that the Absolute Truth consists of the infinite Supreme Being along with the infinitesimal, individual souls.

Gaudiya *sampradaya*--the school of Vaishnavism founded by Sri Caitanya.

Gayatri--the spiritual vibration or *mantra* from which the other *Vedas* were expanded and which is chanted by those who are initiated as *brahmanas* and given the spiritual understanding of Vedic philosophy.

Ghat--a bathing place along a river or lake with steps leading down to the water.

Goloka Vrindavana--the name of Lord Krishna's spiritual planet.

Gosvami--one who is master of the senses.

Govinda--a name of Krishna which means one who gives pleasure to the cows and senses.

Govindaraja--Krishna as Lord of the Cowherds.

Grihastha--the householder order of life. One of the four *ashramas* in spiritual life.

Hare-- the Lord's pleasure potency, Radharani, who is approached for accessibility to the Lord.

Hari--a name of Krishna as the one who takes away one's obstacles on the spiritual path.

Haribol--a word that means to chant the name of the Lord, Hari.

Harinam--refers to the name of the Lord, Hari.

Impersonalism--the view that God has no personality or form, but is only an impersonal force (Brahman) which the individual souls merge back into when released from material existence.

Impersonalist--those who believe God has no personality or form.

Incarnation--the taking on of a body or form.

Japa--the chanting one performs, usually softly, for one's own meditation.

Japa-mala--the string of beads one uses for chanting.

Jiva--the individual soul or living being.

Jivanmukta--a liberated soul, though still in the material body and universe.

Jnana--knowledge which may be material or spiritual.

Jnana-yoga--the process of linking with the Supreme through empirical knowledge and mental speculation.

Jnani--one engaged in *jnana-yoga*, or the process of cultivating knowledge to understand the Absolute.

Kali-yuga--the fourth and present age, the age of quarrel and confusion, which lasts 432,000 years and began 5,000 years ago.

Kalki--future incarnation of Lord Vishnu who appears at the end of Kali-yuga.

Kalpa--a day in the life of Lord Brahma which lasts a thousand cycles of the four *yugas*.

Karma--material actions performed in regard to developing one's position or for future results which produce *karmic* reactions. It is also the reactions one endures from such fruitive activities.

Karma-kanda--the portion of the *Vedas* which primarily deals with recommended fruitive activities for various results.

Karma-yoga--system of yoga for using one's activities for spiritual advancement.

Karmi--the fruitive worker, one who accumulates more *karma*.

Kirtana--chanting or singing the glories of the Lord.

Krishna--the name of the original Supreme Personality of Godhead which means the most attractive and greatest pleasure. He is the source of all other incarnations, such as Vishnu, Rama, Narasimha, Narayana, Buddha.

Krishnaloka--the spiritual planet where Lord Krishna resides.

Kshatriya--the second class of *varna* of society, or occupation of administrative or protective service, such as warrior or military personnel.

Lakshmi--the goddess of fortune and wife of Lord Vishnu.

Lila--pastimes.

Lilavataras--the many incarnations of God who appear to display various spiritual pastimes to attract the conditioned souls in the material world.

Mahabharata--the great epic of the Pandavas, which includes the *Bhagavad-gita*, by Vyasadeva.

Maha-mantra--the best *mantra* for self-realization in this age, called the Hare Krishna *mantra*.

Mandir--a temple.

Mantra--a sound vibration which prepares the mind for spiritual realization and delivers the mind from material inclinations. In some cases a *mantra* is chanted for specific material benefits.

Maya--illusion, or anything that appears to not be connected with the eternal Absolute Truth.

Mayavadi--the impersonalist or voidist who believes that the Supreme has no form, or that any form of God is but a product of *maya*.

Mleccha--a derogatory name for an untouchable person, a meat-eater.

Moksha--liberation from material existence.

Om or *Omkara*--*pranava*, the transcendental *om mantra*, generally referring to the attributeless or impersonal aspects of the Absolute.

Paramahamsa--the highest level of self-realized devotees of the Lord.

Paramatma--the Supersoul, or localized expansion of the Lord in the heart of everyone.

Parampara--the system of disciplic succession through which transcendental knowledge descends.

Pranayama--control of the breathing process as in *astanga* or *raja-yoga*.

Pranava--same as *omkara*.

Prasada--food or other articles that have been offered to the Deity in the temple and then distributed amongst people as the blessings or mercy of the Deity.

Prema--Matured love for Krishna. Pure *rati* at the stage where only the Lord and nothing else is the subject, and is thus suitable for pastimes. When the relationship of love between the couple remains always without destruction even when there are causes for destroying it. When *bhava* become extremely condensed, it is called *prema*. It softens the heart completely and produces extreme possessiveness of the Lord in the experiencer. (BRS 1.4.1)

Puja--the worship offered to the Deity.

Pujari--the priest who performs worship, *puja*, to the Deity.

Radha--Krishna's favorite devotee and the personification of His bliss potency.

Sadhana--a specific practice or discipline for attaining God realization.

Sadhu--Indian holy man or devotee.

Samadhi--trance, the perfection of being absorbed in the Absolute.

Samsara--rounds of life; cycles of birth and death; reincarnation.

Sanatana-dharma--the eternal nature of the living being, to love and render service to the supreme lovable object, the Lord.

Sankirtana-yajna--the prescribed sacrifice for this age: congregational chanting of the holy names of God.

Sannyasa--the renounced order of life, the highest of the four *ashramas* on the spiritual path.

Satya-yuga--the first of the four ages which lasts 1,728,000 years.

Shabda-brahma--the original spiritual vibration or energy of which the *Vedas* are composed.

Shastra--the authentic revealed Vedic scripture.

Shiva--the benevolent one, the demigod who is in charge of the material mode of ignorance and the destruction of the universe. Part of the triad of Brahma, Vishnu, and Shiva who continually create, maintain, and destroy the universe. He is known as Rudra when displaying his destructive aspect.

Smaranam--remembering the Lord.

Smriti--the traditional Vedic knowledge "that is remembered" from what was directly heard by or revealed to the *rishis*.

Sravanam--hearing about the Lord.

Srimad-Bhagavatam--the most ripened fruit of the tree of Vedic knowledge compiled by Vyasadeva.

Sruti--scriptures that were received directly from

God and transmitted orally by *brahmanas* or *rishis* down through succeeding generations. Traditionally, it is considered the four primary *Vedas.*

Sudra--the working class of society, the fourth of the *varnas.*

Svami--one who can control his mind and senses.

Upanishads--the portions of the *Vedas* which primarily explain philosophically the Absolute Truth. It is knowledge of Brahman which releases one from the world and allows one to attain self-realization when received from a qualified teacher. Except for the *Isa Upanishad*, which is the 40th chapter of the *Vajasaneyi Samhita* of the *Sukla* (*White*) *Yajur-veda*, the *Upanishads* are connected to the four primary *Vedas*, generally found in the *Brahmanas.*

Vaikunthas--the planets located in the spiritual sky.

Vaishnava--a worshiper of the Supreme Lord Vishnu or Krishna and His expansions or incarnations.

Vaishnava-*aparadha*--an offense against a Vaisnava or devotee, which can negate all of one's spiritual progress.

Vasudeva--Krishna.

Vedanta-sutras--the philosophical conclusion of the four *Vedas.*

Vedas--generally means the four primary *samhitas;* *Rig, Yajur, Sama, Atharva.*

Vishnu--the expansion of Lord Krishna who enters into the material energy to create and maintain the cosmic world.

Vrindavana--the place where Lord Krishna displayed His village pastimes 5,000 years ago, and is considered to be part of the spiritual abode.

Vyasadeva--the incarnation of God who appeared as the greatest philosopher who compiled the main portions of the Vedic literature into written form.

INDEX

Asanas
  promotes better health ...132
Being spiritual ...132
Bhagavad-gita ...105
  culmination of Upanishad knowledge ...110
  growth and development for everyone ...2
  instructions on yoga .38
  its purpose ...1
  ultimate purpose 105
Bhakti-yoga
  highest of all ...46
Bodily desires ...77
Boundless
  joy and bliss ...6
Brahman ...39
Control of the Mind ...20
Dealing with Stress ...17
Death ...76
  being delivered at the time of ...101
  dealing with ...31
Devotee of God ...97
Devotional service ...88
Diet
  for higher awareness 72
Diligence ...67

Divine nature of God ...91
Example for others ...99
Faith ...61
Fearlessness ...33
Foods for Health ...34
Good Leadership ...14
Good Management ...12
Guru ...71
Happiness and distress .18
Hare Krishna mantra 86
Higher taste of spiritual life ...81
Holy names ...86
Human life
  meant for spiritual inquiry ...2
Improvement in character ...69
Karma-yoga ...4
Knowledge
  how to acquire ...36
Krishna
  comes to deliver the pious ...92
  the Supreme Being ...10
Kurukshetra ...106, 113
Life after death ...80
Meat
  a product of violence 73
Meditation ...38
Mental platform ...78

Modes or gunas 8
Moksha Liberation 59
Moksha-Liberation 87
Nature of the soul 53
Paramatma 40
Peace of mind 23
Power of God 92
Prasada
   sacred food 73
Purpose 27
Purpose of life 66
Qualities
   for the higher good ... 68
Raja yoga
   difficulties in it 44
Raja-yoga 38
Real education 63
Self-confidence 26
Sharing this message .. 102
Soul 74
   beyond the body 8
   is eternal 76
Spiritual enlightenment 52

Spiritual joys 24
Spiritual purification 66
Spiritual vision 53
Supersoul
   plenary expansion of
   God 39
Supreme Yoga 46
Threefold miseries 18
Tolerance 95
Transcendental
   knowledge 63
Transcendentalist
   results of one who fails
   45
Unsuccessful yogi 45
Unsuccessful Yogi 44
Work done for Vishnu . 83
Work Ethics 16
World Peace 55
Yoga
   benefits 132
Yogi
   who is unsuccessful . 45

ABOUT THE AUTHOR

Stephen Knapp grew up in a Christian family, during which time he seriously studied the Bible to understand its teachings. In his late teenage years, however, he sought answers to questions not easily explained in Christian theology. So he began to search through other religions and philosophies from around the world and started to find the answers for which he was looking. He also studied a variety of occult sciences, ancient mythology, mysticism, yoga, and the spiritual teachings of the East. After his first reading of the *Bhagavad-gita*, he felt he had found the last piece of the puzzle he had been putting together through all of his research. Therefore, he continued to study all of the major Vedic texts of India to gain a better understanding of the Vedic science.

It is known amongst all Eastern mystics that anyone, regardless of qualifications, academic or otherwise, who does not engage in the spiritual practices described in the Vedic texts cannot actually enter into understanding the depths of the Vedic spiritual science, nor acquire the realizations that should accompany it. So, rather than pursuing his research in an academic atmosphere at a university, Stephen directly engaged in the spiritual disciplines that have been recommended for hundreds of years. He continued his study of Vedic knowledge and spiritual practice under the guidance of a spiritual master. Through this process, and with the sanction of His Divine Grace A. C. Bhaktivedanta Swami Prabhupada, he became initiated into the genuine and authorized spiritual line of the Brahma-Madhava-Gaudiya *sampradaya*, which is a disciplic succession that descends back through Sri Caitanya Mahaprabhu and Sri Vyasadeva, the compiler of

Vedic literature, and further back to Sri Krishna. At that time he was given the spiritual name of Sri Nandanandana dasa. In this way, he has been studying and practicing yoga since 1971, especially bhakti-yoga, and has attained many insights and realizations through this means. Besides being *brahminically* initiated, Stephen has also been to India more than 20 times and traveled extensively throughout the country, visiting most of the major holy places and gaining a wide variety of spiritual experiences that only such places can give. He has also spent nearly 40 years in the management of various Krishna temples.

Stephen has put the culmination of nearly 50 years of continuous research and travel experience into his books in an effort to share it with those who are also looking for spiritual understanding. More books are forthcoming, so stay in touch through his website to find out further developments.

More information about Stephen, his projects, books, free ebooks, and numerous articles and videos can be found on his website at: www.stephen-knapp.com or http://stephenknapp.info or his blog at http://stephenknapp.wordpress.com.

Stephen has continued to write books that include in *The Eastern Answers to the Mysteries of Life* series:
1. *The Secret Teachings of the Vedas: The Eastern Answers to the Mysteries of Life*
2. *The Universal Path to Enlightenment*
3. *The Vedic Prophecies: A New Look into the Future*
4. *How the Universe was Created and Our Purpose In It*
   He has also written:
5. *Toward World Peace: Seeing the Unity Between Us All*
6. *Facing Death: Welcoming the Afterlife*
7. *The Key to Real Happiness*
8. *Proof of Vedic Culture's Global Existence*
9. *The Heart of Hinduism: The Eastern Path to Freedom, Enlightenment and Illumination*

10. *The Power of the Dharma: An Introduction to Hinduism and Vedic Culture*
11. *Vedic Culture: The Difference it can Make in Your Life*
12. *Reincarnation & Karma: How They Really Affect Us*
13. *The Eleventh Commandment: The Next Step for Social Spiritual Development*
14. *Seeing Spiritual India: A Guide to Temples, Holy Sites, Festivals and Traditions*
15. *Crimes Against India: And the Need to Protect its Ancient Vedic Tradition*
16. *Yoga and Meditation: Their Real Purpose and How to Get Started*
17. *Avatars, Gods and Goddesses of Vedic Culture: Understanding the Characteristics, Powers and Positions of the Hindu Divinities*
18. *The Soul: Understanding Our Real Identity*
19. *Prayers, Mantras and Gayatris: A Collection for Insights, Protection, Spiritual Growth, and Many Other Blessings*
20. *Krishna Deities and Their Miracles: How the Images of Lord Krishna Interact with Their Devotees*
21. *Defending Vedic Dharma: Tackling the Issues to Make a Difference*
22. *Advancements of the Ancient Vedic Culture*
23. *Spreading Vedic Traditions Through Temples*
24. *The Bhakti-yoga Handbook*
25. *Lord Krishna and His Essential Teachings*
26. *Mysteries of the Ancient Vedic Empire*
27. *Casteism in India*
28. *Ancient History of Vedic Culture*
29. *A Complete Review of Vedic Literature*
30. *Destined for Infinity*, an exciting novel for those who prefer lighter reading, or learning spiritual knowledge in the context of an action oriented, spiritual adventure.
31. *Bhakti-Yoga: The Easy Path of Devotional Yoga.*
32. *The Power of the Maha-Mantra.*

BOOKS BY STEPHEN KNAPP

If you have enjoyed this book, or if you are serious about finding higher levels of real spiritual Truth, and learning more about the mysteries of India's Vedic culture, then you will also want to get other books written by Stephen Knapp, a few of which include:

The Power of the Dharma
An Introduction to Hinduism and Vedic Culture

The Power of the Dharma offers you a concise and easy-to-understand overview of the essential principles and customs of Hinduism and the reasons for them. It provides many insights into the depth and value of the timeless wisdom of Vedic spirituality and why the Dharmic path has survived for so many hundreds of years. It reveals why the Dharma is presently enjoying a renaissance of an increasing number of interested people who are exploring its teachings and seeing what its many techniques of Self-discovery have to offer.

Herein you will find:
- Quotes by noteworthy people on the unique qualities of Hinduism
- Essential principles of the Vedic spiritual path
- Particular traits and customs of Hindu worship and explanations of them
- Descriptions of the main Yoga systems
- The significance and legends of the colorful Hindu festivals
- Benefits of Ayurveda, Vastu, Vedic astrology and gemology,
- Important insights of Dharmic life and how to begin.

The Dharmic path can provide you the means for attaining your own spiritual realizations and experiences. In this way it is as relevant today as it was thousands of years ago. This is the power of the Dharma since its universal teachings have something to offer anyone.

Published by iUniverse.com, 170 pages, 6" x 9" trim size, $16.95, ISBN: 0-595-39352-7.

The Bhakti-yoga Handbook
A Guide for Beginning the Essentials of Devotional Yoga

This book is a guide for anyone who wants to begin the practice of bhakti-yoga in a practical and effective way. This supplies the information, the principles, the regular activities or *sadhana*, and how to have the right attitude in applying ourselves to attain success on the path of bhakti-yoga, which is uniting with God through love and devotion.

This outlines a general schedule for our daily spiritual activities and a typical morning program as found in most Krishna temples that are centered around devotional yoga. In this way, you will find the explanations on how to begin our day and set our mind, what meditations to do, which spiritual texts are best to study, and how we can make most everything we do as part of bhakti-yoga. All of these can be adjusted in a way that can be practiced and applied by anyone by anyone regardless of whether you are in a temple ashrama or in your own home or apartment.

Such topics include:
- The secret of bhakti-yoga and its potency in this day and age,
- The essential morning practice, the best time for meditation,
- The standard songs and mantras that we can use, as applied in most Krishna temples,
- Understanding the basics of the Vedic spiritual philosophy, such as karma, reincarnation, the Vedic description of the soul, etc.,
- How Vedic culture is still as relevant today as ever,
- Who is Sri Krishna,
- How to chant the Hare Krishna mantra,
- Standards for temple etiquette,
- The nine processes of bhakti-yoga, a variety of activities from which anyone can utilize,
- How to make our career a part of the yoga process,
- How to turn our cooking into bhakti-yoga,
- How to set up a home altar or temple room, depending on what standard you wish to establish,
- How to take care of deities in our home, if we have Them,
- How to perform the basic ceremonies like arati,

All of the basics and effective applications to get started and continue with your practice of bhakti-yoga is supplied so you can progress in a steady way, from beginner to advanced.

This is 278 pages, $14.95, ISBN: 149030228X.

Bhakti Yoga: The Easy Path of Devotional Yoga

This is a systematic description of how bhakti-yoga works, the practice and philosophy of it, and how to become successful on this spiritual path.

Bhakti-yoga is the process that can take a person beyond mere faith and give direct experience of the spiritual strata and one's real spiritual identity, beyond the body, and to the joy that is on that plane of consciousness. It is the spiritual process that is especially recommended for these difficult times.

Herein is a revelation that such a realization and experience is not only possible, but leads us to taste the greatest happiness when the soul finally reconnects to its natural condition and joyful disposition. It is like finding the home you have been looking for all your life. And now, at long last, you can reach the ultimate platform of realization, peace, comfort, bliss, and connection with Divine Love. The hankering for this has motivated all of us to seek out our real spiritual nature for many lifetimes, and now upon attaining this knowledge we have found our real destiny. Some of the additional topics within include:

- What is so special about bhakti-yoga, the universal path.
- Mantra-yoga, the importance of it in this day and age.
- How to make sure you have a genuine guru.
- Feeling ecstatic reciprocation from the Lord.
- Beginning to understand and perceive God.
- How the Lord reveals Himself to His devotee.
- Having your own realizations of the highest levels of spiritual truth.
- Manifesting your spiritual identity.
- And ultimately attaining freedom from material existence and entering the spiritual world.

This book is based on and includes numerous quotes and references from the Vedic literature to authorize the knowledge that is presented within.

This is 460 pages, $20.95, ISBN: 1977610196.

The Power of the Maha-Mantra

There are certain channels through which the higher spiritual frequencies become approachable by humanity, and by which the Infinite descends into this world. One channel is through transcendental sound. The Hare Krishna *Maha-mantra* is one such channel of pure spiritual vibration. The mantra is therefore a point of meditation for the mind, but also a formula or transcendental sound vibration that releases its energy into one's consciousness. Thus it can prepare a person for perceiving higher states of reality. With continued practice with this mantra, and with the proper devotional mood, the mantra can uplift our mind in many ways, help us rise above bad habits and thought patterns, and can even reveal the Absolute Truth to the practitioner. It can also show one's own spiritual identity and relationship that you have with the Supreme Being.

Additional topics in this book include:
- How Mantra-Yoga is a necessity for this age.
- How to chant Om properly.
- How the Maha-mantra works and what makes it so effective.
- The meaning and significance of the Maha-mantra.
- How spiritual realization can be attained through chanting the Maha-mantra.
- The great good fortune of those who chant the Maha-mantra, and the bliss found in chanting it.
- How to attain the spiritual world through the Maha-mantra.
- How to practice the chanting of the Maha-mantra to release its fullest potential.

This book will help open the spiritual possibilities as well as bliss that you can attain through the simple process of chanting the Hare Krishna Maha-mantra.

This is 150 pages, $9.95, ISBN: 1983873489.

Yoga and Meditation Their Real Purpose and How to Get Started

Yoga is a nonsectarian spiritual science that has been practiced and developed over thousands of years. The benefits of yoga are numerous. On the mental level it strengthens concentration, determination, and builds a stronger character that can more easily sustain various tensions in our lives for peace of mind. The assortment of *asanas* or postures also provide stronger health and keeps various diseases in check. They improve physical strength, endurance and flexibility. These are some of the goals of yoga.

Its ultimate purpose is to raise our consciousness to directly perceive the spiritual dimension. Then we can have our own spiritual experiences. The point is that the more spiritual we become, the more we can perceive that which is spiritual. As we develop and grow in this way through yoga, the questions about spiritual life are no longer a mystery to solve, but become a reality to experience. It becomes a practical part of our lives. This book will show you how to do that. Some of the topics include:

- Benefits of yoga
- The real purpose of yoga
- The types of yoga, such as Hatha yoga, Karma yoga, Raja and Astanga yogas, Kundalini yoga, Bhakti yoga, Mudra yoga, Mantra yoga, and others.
- The Chakras and Koshas
- Asanas and postures, and the Surya Namaskar
- Pranayama and breathing techniques for inner changes
- Deep meditation and how to proceed
- The methods for using mantras
- Attaining spiritual enlightenment, and much more

This book is 6"x9" trim size, $17.95, 240 pages, 32 illustration, ISBN: 1451553269.

Avatars, Gods and Goddesses of Vedic Culture

The Characteristics, Powers and Positions of the Hindu Divinities

Understanding the assorted Divinities or gods and goddesses of the Vedic or Hindu pantheon is not so difficult as some people may think when it is presented simply and effectively. And that is what you will find in this book. This will open you to many of the possibilities and potentials of the Vedic tradition, and show how it has been able to cater to and fulfill the spiritual needs and development of so many people since time immemorial. Here you will find there is something for everyone.

This takes you into the heart of the deep, Vedic spiritual knowledge of how to perceive the Absolute Truth, the Supreme and the various powers and agents of the universal creation. This explains the characteristics and nature of the Vedic Divinities and their purposes, powers, and the ways they influence and affect the natural energies of the universe. It also shows how they can assist us and that blessings from them can help our own spiritual and material development and potentialities, depending on what we need.

Some of the Vedic Divinities that will be explained include Lord Krishna, Vishnu, Their main avatars and expansions, along with Brahma, Shiva, Ganesh, Murugan, Surya, Hanuman, as well as the goddesses of Sri Radha, Durga, Sarasvati, Lakshmi, and others. This also presents explanations of their names, attributes, dress, weapons, instruments, the meaning of the Shiva lingam, and some of the legends and stories that are connected with them. This will certainly give you a new insight into the expansive nature of the Vedic tradition.

This book is: $17.95 retail, 230 pages, 11 black & white photos, ISBN: 1453613765, EAN: 9781453613764.

The Soul
Understanding Our Real Identity
The Key to Spiritual Awakening

This book provides a summarization of the most essential spiritual knowledge that will give you the key to spiritual awakening. The descriptions will give you greater insights and a new look at who and what you really are as a spiritual being.

The idea that we are more than merely these material bodies is pervasive. It is established in every religion and spiritual path in this world. However, many religions only hint at the details of this knowledge, but if we look around we will find that practically the deepest and clearest descriptions of the soul and its characteristics are found in the ancient Vedic texts of India.

Herein you will find some of the most insightful spiritual knowledge and wisdom known to mankind. Some of the topics include:

- How you are more than your body
- The purpose of life
- Spiritual ignorance of the soul is the basis of illusion and suffering
- The path of spiritual realization
- How the soul is eternal
- The unbounded nature of the soul
- What is the Supersoul
- Attaining direct spiritual perception and experience of our real identity

This book will give you a deeper look into the ancient wisdom of India's Vedic, spiritual culture, and the means to recognize your real identity.

This book is 5 1/2"x8 1/2" trim size, 130 pages, $7.95, ISBN: 1453733833.

The Eleventh Commandment
The Next Step in Social Spiritual Development

A New Code to Bring Humanity to a Higher Level of Spiritual Consciousness

This is some of Stephen's boldest and most direct writing. Based on the Universal Spiritual Truths, or the deeper levels of spiritual understanding, it presents a new code in a completely nonsectarian way that anyone should be able and willing to follow. Herein is the next step for consideration, which can be used as a tool for guidance, and for setting a higher standard in our society today. This new commandment expects and directs us toward a change in our social awareness and spiritual consciousness. It is conceived, formulated, and now provided to assist humanity in reaching its true destiny, and to bring a new spiritual dimension into the basic fabric of our ordinary every day life. It is a key that unlocks the doors of perception, and opens up a whole new aspect of spiritual understanding for all of us to view. It is the commandment which precepts us to gain the knowledge of the hidden mysteries, which have for so long remained an enigma to the confused and misdirected men of this world. It holds the key which unlocks the answers to man's quest for peace and happiness, and the next step for spiritual growth on a dynamic and all-inclusive social level.

This 11th Commandment and the explanations provided show the means for curing social ills, reducing racial prejudices, and create more harmony between the races and cultures. It shows how to recognize the Divine within yourself and all beings around you. It shows how we can bring some of the spiritual atmosphere into this earthly existence, especially if we expect to reach the higher domain after death.

It also explains how to:
- Identify our real Self and distinguish it from our false self.
- Open our hearts to one another and view others with greater appreciation.
- Utilize higher consciousness in everyday life.
- Find inner contentment and joy.
- Attain a higher spiritual awareness and perception.
- Manifest God's plan for the world.

- Be a reflection of God's love toward everyone.
- Attain the Great Realization of perceiving the Divine in all beings.

The world is in need of a new direction in its spiritual development, and this 11th Commandment is given as the next phase to manifest humanity's most elevated potentials.

This book is $13.95, Size: 6" x 9", Pages: 128, ISBN: 0-595-46741-5.

www.Stephen-Knapp.com
http://stephenknapp.info
http://stephenknapp.wordpress.com

Be sure to visit Stephen's web site. It provides lots of information on many spiritual aspects of Vedic and spiritual philosophy, and Indian culture for both beginners and the scholarly. You will find:

- All the descriptions and contents of Stephen's books, how to order them, and keep up with any new books or articles that he has written.
- Reviews and unsolicited letters from readers who have expressed their appreciation for his books, as well as his website.
- Free online booklets are also available for your use or distribution on meditation, why be a Hindu, how to start yoga, meditation, etc.
- Helpful prayers, mantras, gayatris, and devotional songs.
- Over two hundred enlightening articles that can help answer many questions about life, the process of spiritual development, the basics of the Vedic path, or how to broaden our spiritual awareness.
- Over 150 color photos taken by Stephen during his travels through India. There are also descriptions and 40 photos of the huge and amazing Kumbha Mela festival.
- Directories of many Krishna and Hindu temples around the world to help you locate one near you, where you can continue your experience along the Eastern path.
- Photographic exhibit of the Vedic influence in the Taj Mahal, questioning whether it was built by Shah Jahan or a pre-existing Vedic building.
- A large list of links to additional websites to help you continue your exploration of Eastern philosophy, or provide more information and news about India, Hinduism, ancient Vedic culture, Vaishnavism, Hare Krishna sites, travel, visas, catalogs for books and paraphernalia, holy places, etc.
- A large resource for vegetarian recipes, information on its benefits, how to get started, ethnic stores, or non-meat ingredients and supplies.
- A large "Krishna Darshan Art Gallery" of photos and prints of Krishna and Vedic divinities.
- This site is made as a practical resource for your use and is continually being updated and expanded with more articles, resources, and information. Be sure to check it out.

Printed in Great Britain
by Amazon